One-Skein Wonders

101
Yarn-Shop Favorites

Edited by Judith Durant

Storey Publishing

*For the yarn shops and knitting groups worldwide
who share the love of fibers — and who can never
resist acquiring just one more ball of yarn.*

*The mission of Storey Publishing is to serve our customers by publishing practical information
that encourages personal independence in harmony with the environment.*

Edited by Judith Durant and Gwen Steege
Technical editing by Dorothy T. Ratigan
Art direction and cover design by Mary Velgos
Book design and production by Kate Basart/Union Pageworks
Photography © by 2C imagery
Illustrations by Alison Kolesar
Indexed by Mary McClintock

The information in this book is true and complete to the best of our knowledge. All recommendations are made without guarantee on the part of the editor or Storey Publishing. The editor and publisher disclaim any liability in connection with the use of this information. For additional information, please contact Storey Publishing, 210 MASS MoCA Way, North Adams, MA 01247.

Storey books are available for special premium and promotional uses and for customized editions. For further information, please call 1-800-793-9396.

Printed in the United States by CJK

10 9 8 7 6 5 4 3 2 1

Library of Congress Cataloging-in-Publication Data

One-skein wonders : 101 yarn shop favorites / edited by Judith Durant and Gwen Steege
    p. cm.
Includes bibliographical references and index.
    ISBN-13: 978-1-58017-645-3; ISBN-10: 1-58017-645-3 (pbk. : alk. paper)
    1. Knitting—Patterns. I. Durant, Judith, 1955– II. Steege, Gwen, 1940–
TT820.O55 2006
746.43'2041—dc22

                  2006023060

Contents

For Better or Worsted: Worsted-Weight Yarns 61

Gallery of Projects: Picture This 97

Introduction: Have a Ball!

This book has been created for all those knitters and crocheters who find themselves with just one ball or skein of very special yarn but only a vague idea of what to do with it. Maybe you just couldn't resist a certain perfect color or texture—or bargain. Or maybe the yarn wasn't a bargain—in fact, it was terribly expensive, but still irresistible and buying just one seemed okay! Your one skein could also be part of that famous (or infamous) stash: yarns you've been saving for a special occasion or well-loved leftovers that are still waiting for just the right project.

The patterns chosen for this collection have been generously shared by yarn shops and designers who have met this challenge with creativity and enthusiasm. (See pages 221–227 for information about all the wonderful contributors.) From quick-and-easy projects knit with thick yarns on fat needles to those worked in the finest of lace-weights, there's something for every knitter and every occasion. Each pattern specifies the yarn used by the designer for the item photographed for the book. You can purchase that yarn for an exact replica or use your own yarn of choice. Browse through the 101 patterns in the pages that follow and let yourself be tempted and inspired by projects that will consume both your stash and your passion for knitting!

Note: Refer to the Glossary (pages 228–235) for any unfamiliar terms or abbreviations.

vi

In the Thick of It:
Bulky-Weight Yarns

One-Car-Ride Coaster Set

Photo, p. 97

Designed by
Sarah Marie Fuchs

Submitted by
Bella Filati Luxury Yarns
Southern Pines, NC

These felted coasters couldn't be easier. Cast on, knit, bind off, felt. That's it! The fun part of this project is the needle felting (designed by Ryan Anderson), which uses up bits and pieces of leftover wool. The knitting part is "mindless," the decorating part is creative. The best of both worlds.

MEASUREMENTS	3" (7.5 cm) wide and 3.25" (8.5 cm) tall, felted (*Note:* Exact finished measurements will be determined by the yarn and the point at which you stop felting.)
YARN	JCA Reynolds Lopi, 100% Icelandic wool, 3.5 oz (100 g)/110 yd (100 m) (*Note:* One skein will make two sets of five coasters.)
NEEDLES	US 10 or 10.5 (6–6.5 mm) straight needles or size you need to obtain correct gauge
GAUGE	13–14 stitches = 4" (10 cm) in garter stitch
OTHER SUPPLIES	Needle Felting starter kit and scraps of wool yarn, optional

Knitting

Cast on 11 stitches. Work garter stitch for 20 rows.

Bind off. Weave in ends.

Felting

Place coasters in washing machine with hot water and heavy clothing such as jeans to help with agitation. Check coasters every few minutes. When the stitches are no longer visible, the coasters are done. Dry completely.

Needle Felting

Lay scrap yarn on coaster in desired pattern. Using felting needles, "stab" the yarn into position until it has adhered. (Felting kits come with instructions on how to needle-felt.)

Shepherd Bulky Rainbow Hat·············

Photo, p. 99

This hat is knitted in three directions. First you knit the cuff from center back to center back. Then you pick up the top of the cuff and knit up to the center of the crown. Then you pick up the bottom and knit down for the edging. Every which way!

Designed by
Bobbe Morris

Submitted by
Haus of Yarn
Nashville, TN

MEASUREMENTS	Approximately 20" (51 cm) circumference
YARN	Lorna's Laces Shepherd Bulky, 100% superwash wool, 3.5 oz (100 g)/140 yds (128 m), Seaside
NEEDLES	US 10 (6 mm) straight needles and one US 10 (6 mm) circular needle 16" (40 cm) long or size you need to obtain correct gauge
GAUGE	14 stitches = 4" (10 cm) in pattern
ABBREVIATIONS	C4F Cable 4 front (see at right)

Knitting the Cuff

Cast on 25 stitches.

Row 1: K2, P1, K1, (P2, K4, P2, K1) twice, P1, K2.

Row 2: (K1, P1) twice, (K2, P4, K2, P1) twice, K1, P1, K1.

Row 3: K2, P1, K1, (P2, C4F, P2, K1) twice, P1, K2.

Row 4: Repeat Row 2.

Repeat Rows 1–4 until piece measures 20", ending with Row 4.

Bind off in pattern.

Cable 4 Front

Slip 2 stitches onto cable needle and hold in front. Knit the next 2 stitches, then knit the 2 stitches from cable needle.

Beginning the Top

With right side of cuff facing you, pick up and knit 74 stitches along one side of cuff edge.

Row 1 (wrong side): P9, (K1, P8) seven times, K1, P1.

Row 2: K1, (P1, K8) eight times, K1.

Repeat Rows 1 and 2 for 1.5", ending with Row 2.

Shaping the Top

Row 1: P1, (P6, P2tog, K1) eight times, P1. You now have 66 stitches.

Row 2 and all even-numbered rows: Knit the knits and purl the purls (see Glossary, page 230).

Row 3: P1, (P5, P2tog, K1) eight times, P1. You now have 58 stitches.

Row 5: P1, (P4, P2tog, K1) eight times, P1. You now have 50 stitches.

Continue in this manner, decreasing 8 stitches every other row, until 26 stitches remain.

Next Row: P1, (P2tog, K1) eight times, P1.

Break yarn, leaving a 12" tail. Thread tail onto tapestry needle and draw through remaining 18 stitches. Pull up snug and fasten off on the inside.

Sew back seam.

Knitting the Edging

With right side facing you, pick up and knit 70 stitches along bottom edge. Knit 4–8 rounds, making sure you leave enough yarn to bind off. Bind off loosely and let edge roll up.

Finishing

Weave in ends.

One-Skein-Wonder Baby Sweater ....

This cozy baby cardigan will knit up fast in bulky yarn on size 10.5 needles. And the best part is that there is little finishing to be done. The only pieces to join are the shoulder seams. And you don't even have to make buttonholes—the stitches are large enough to accommodate the buttons!

Photo, p. 97

Designed by
Linda Burt

Submitted by
Webs
Northampton, MA

MEASUREMENTS	Infant (0–12 months), 23" (58.5 cm) chest
YARN	Valley Yarns, Kangaroo Dyer Dover, 100% wool, 8 oz (227 g)/336 yds (307 m), Pumpkin Patch
NEEDLES	US 10.5 (6.5 mm) straight needles and set of US 10.5 (6.5 mm) double-point needles or size you need to obtain correct gauge
GAUGE	12 stitches = 4" (10 cm) in stockinette stitch
OTHER SUPPLIES	Stitch holders, four buttons ⅝–⅞" (1.5–2.2 cm)

Getting Started

With straight needles, cast on 72 stitches. Knit 2 rows.

Keeping 2 stitches at each end of needle in garter stitch, change to stockinette stitch and work until piece measures 5.5" from beginning, ending with a wrong-side row.

Dividing for Front and Back

Knit 19 and place on holder, knit 34, knit 19 and place on holder. Working 34 back stitches only, knit in stockinette stitch until piece measures 11" from beginning. Cut yarn and place stitches on holder.

Knitting the Right Front

With right side facing, place right front stitches onto straight needles. Keeping the two center front stitches in garter, knit in stockinette stitch until piece measures 9.5" from beginning, ending with a wrong-side row.

Bind off 7 stitches at beginning of next row, knit to end.

Purl 1 row. Bind off 3 stitches at beginning of next row, knit to end.

Purl 1 row.

Work even until piece measures 11" from beginning. Cut yarn and place stitches on holder.

Knitting the Left Front

With right-side facing, place left front stitches onto straight needles. Keeping the 2 center front stitches in garter, knit in stockinette stitch until piece measures 9.5" from beginning, ending with a right-side row.

Bind off 7 stitches at beginning of next row, purl to end.

Knit 1 row.

Bind off 3 stitches at beginning of next row, purl to end.

Knit 1 row.

Work even until piece measures 11" from beginning.

Joining the Shoulders

With right sides together, join 8 front and back shoulder stitches on both sides using the three-needle bind-off (see Glossary, page 235). Leave remaining back neck stitches on holder.

Knitting the Sleeves (make 2)

With double-point needles, pick up 34 stitches around sleeve opening and distribute evenly on three needles with first picked-up stitch at beginning of Needle 1 and last picked-up stitch at end of Needle 3.

Knit 5 rows.

Decrease 1 stitch at beginning and end of next row, then every 4 rows four times, then every 2 rows once. You now have 22 stitches.

Work even until sleeve measures 6.5" from beginning.

Purl 1 row, knit 1 row.

Bind off in purl.

Knitting the Collar

With straight needles and right side facing, skip 3 stitches, pick up 9 stitches along right-front neck edge, knit the 34 back neck stitches, pick up 9 stitches along left-front neck edge to within 3 stitches of center front. Work in garter stitch until collar measures 3". Bind off.

Finishing

Weave in ends. Block. Sew on buttons.

Doll Shawl······················

The small shawl is the same pattern as the Seafoam Shawl on page 59. It is quick and easy and an excellent project for a child to make for her doll. One skein yields two Aran sweaters and one shawl for an 18" doll.

MEASUREMENTS	Approximately 15" (38 cm) wide and 8" (20.5 cm) long
YARN	Kerry Woollen Mills Aran Wool, 100% wool, 7 oz (200 g)/350 yds (320 m), Light Jacob
NEEDLES	US 9 (5.25 mm) straight needles or size you need to obtain correct gauge
GAUGE	Approximately 12 stitches = 4" (10 cm) in pattern
OTHER SUPPLIES	½" (1.3 cm) button

Photo, p. 112

Designed by
Nancy Miller

Submitted by
KnitWit Yarn Shop
Portland, ME

In the Thick of It: Bulky-Weight Yarns

Knitting the Shawl

Cast on 2 stitches, leaving a tail of approximately 2 inches.

Row 1: K1, yo, K1.

Row 2 and all even rows: Knit.

Row 3: K1, yo, knit to last stitch, yo, K1.

Repeat Rows 2 and 3 until shawl measures 8", leaving enough yarn for 2 more rows plus bind-off.

Next Row: Kfb, *yo, K2tog; repeat from* to last 2 stitches, yo, Kfb, K1.

Knit 1 row and bind off.

Finishing

Weave in ends. Sew button on left front and use a yarnover space as a buttonhole.

Flap Hat

Here's a quick-to-knit version of a classic hat. Sure to keep you warm in even the coldest temperatures, the earflaps are at once practical and fun.

Photo, p.111

Designed by
Sue Coffrin

Submitted by
Adirondack Yarns
Lake Placid, NY

MEASUREMENTS	18" (45.5 cm) circumference
YARN	Brown Sheep Company Burly Spun, 100% wool, 8 oz (227 g)/132 yds (120 m)
NEEDLES	One US 13 (9 mm) circular needle 16" (40 cm) long and set of US 13 (9 mm) double-point needles or size you need to obtain correct gauge
GAUGE	9 stitches = 4" (10 cm) in stockinette stitch
OTHER SUPPLIES	Tapestry needle

Knitting the Band

With circular needle, cast on 42 stitches. Join into a round, being careful not to twist stitches.

Work K1, P1 rib for 1.5".

Knitting the Hat

Knit 1 round, increasing 2 stitches evenly spaced. You now have 44 stitches.

Work stockinette stitch (knit every round) until hat measures 5.25" from beginning.

Decreasing for the Crown

Decrease Round 1: K2, *K4, K2tog; repeat from *. You now have 37 stitches.

Knit 1 round.

Decrease Round 2: K2, *K3, K2tog; repeat from *. You now have 30 stitches.

Knit 1 round.

Decrease Round 3: K2, *K2, K2tog; repeat from *. You now have 23 stitches.

Knit 1 round.

Decrease Round 4: K2, *K1, K2tog; repeat from *. You now have 16 stitches.

Knit 1 round.

Last Decrease Round: *K2tog; repeat from *. You now have 8 stitches.

Cut yarn, leaving a 10" tail. Thread tail onto tapestry needle, draw through remaining 8 stitches. Pull up snug and fasten off on the inside.

Knitting the Earflaps

With double-point needles, pick up and knit 9 stitches along cast-on edge.

Knit 4 rows.

Decrease Row: K2tog, K5, K2tog. You now have 7 stitches.

Knit 1 row.

Repeat these 2 rows until 3 stitches remain.

Work 3-stitch I-cord (see Glossary, page 229) to desired length.

Bind off.

Fold hat in half and pick up 9 stitches exactly opposite this earflap and work second earflap as above.

Finishing

Weave in ends.

Photo, p. 115

Designed by
Tatyana Tchibova

Submitted by
Hilltop Yarn
Seattle, WA

·······Super Yak Scarf

This pattern uses a unique stitch: Make 7, which means you make seven stitches out of one. This not only creates the necessary stitches for the pattern, but it also produces a lovely eyelet at its base. It's not just the yarn that will have your friends "yakking" about this scarf!

MEASUREMENTS	Approximately 5" (12.5 cm) wide and 34" (86.5 cm) long
YARN	Karabella Super Yak, 50% yak/50% extrafine merino wool, 1.75 oz (50 g)/125 yds (114 m), Color 10397
NEEDLES	US 10 (6 mm) straight needles or size you need to obtain correct gauge
GAUGE	16 stitches and 21 rows = 4" (10 cm) in pattern
ABBREVIATIONS	M7 Make 7 in the next stitch (see facing page)

Knitting the First Ruffle

Cast on 51 stitches.

Rows 1, 3, 5, 6, and 7 (wrong side): Knit.

Row 2: *K1, K2tog; repeat from *. You now have 34 stitches.

Row 4: K2, *K2tog; repeat from * to last 2 stitches, K2. You now have 19 stitches.

Knitting the Body

Row 1 (RS): K3, P4, P2tog, Make 7, P2tog, P4, K3. You now have 23 stitches.

Continue by following the chart below, beginning with Row 2.

Work Rows 1–10 of chart 16 times total.

Next Row (WS): K3, P4, P2tog, P1, P2tog, P4, K3. You now have 17 stitches.

Working the Second Ruffle

Knit 3 rows.

Next Row: *Kfb; repeat from *. You now have 34 stitches.

Knit 1 row.

Next Row: *K1, Kfb; repeat from *. You now have 51 stitches.

Knit 1 row.

Bind off.

Finishing

Weave in ends. Block if desired.

Key	
☐	knit on RS; purl on WS
•	purl on RS; knit on WS
⟋	purl 2 together
⩔	Make 7; k1, (yo, k1) 3 times
o	yarn over
⟋	knit 2 together
⟍	slip, slip, knit 2 together
⋀	slip 1 as to knit, knit 2 tog, pass the slip stitch over
▨	no stitch

Make 7

To make 7 stitches in the next stitch, work as follows: K1, yo, K1, yo, K1, yo, K1.

Felted Accessory Bag

Use this attractive little bag to pack your jewelry when traveling, to hold together your scissors and other accessories in your knitting bag, or for any number of other things for which small organizers come in handy. Consider the bulkier bag for larger items.

Photo, p.106

Designed by
Marlee Mason

Submitted by
Stitchy Women
Poultney, VT

MEASUREMENTS	Approximately 8" (20.5 cm) wide and 5.75" (14.5 cm) tall, before felting; approximately 6" (15 cm) wide and 4" (10 cm) tall after felting (*Note:* Exact finished measurements will be determined by the yarn and the point at which you stop felting.)
YARN	Crystal Palace Iceland, 100% wool, 3.5 oz (100 g)/109 yds (100 m), 9628 Periwinkle
NEEDLES	One US 11 (8 mm) circular needle 16" (40 cm) long and set of US 7 (4.5 mm) double-point needles or size you need to obtain correct gauge
GAUGE	16 stitches = 4" (10 cm) before felting
OTHER SUPPLIES	One button for closure

Knitting the Bag

With circular needle, cast on 50 stitches. Knit one row and join into a round, being careful not to twist stitches.

Knit 30 rows. Bind off.

Sew bottom edges together.

Felting the Bag

Set the washer for the lowest water level, longest washing cycle, and hottest temperature. Add a small amount of detergent. Place bag in a zippered pillowcase and close. Place in washer with a pair of jeans or heavy towel to balance the load. Run machine on wash cycle only, checking felting status every 5 minutes. If necessary, reset the machine to wash cycle and agitate again. When desired effect is reached, run bag through cold rinse cycle to remove detergent, then through a spin cycle to remove excess water.

Fill the damp bag with towels to shape and allow to dry.

Making the Closure

With double-point needles, cast on 4 stitches.

Work 4-stitch I cord (see Glossary, page 229) for desired length (5–7"). Bind off.

Sew both ends of the strap to the center top of one edge of the felted bag. Attach button where end of loop meets front of bag.

Optional Bulkier Bag

MEASUREMENTS   Approximately 9.75" (25 cm) wide and 6.5" (16.5 cm) tall before felting; approximately 7.5" (19 cm) wide and 5.5" (14 cm) tall after felting

GAUGE   12 stitches = 4" (10 cm) before felting

Follow the same instructions as above with bulkier yarn for a slightly larger, thicker bag.

Fringed Scarf ·············

The Thick 'n Thin yarn used for this scarf feels like the best of two worlds: It has the texture and fun of popular novelty yarn and the earthy feel of homespun wool.

MEASUREMENTS   Approximately 3" (7.5 cm) wide and 75" (190.5 cm) long, with fringe

YARN   Rio Grande Thick 'n Thin, 100% wool, 4 oz (113 g)/122 yds (112 m), Camouflage

NEEDLES   US 17 (12 mm) straight needles or size you need to obtain correct gauge

GAUGE   12 stitches = 4" (10 cm) in pattern

OTHER SUPPLIES   One US K/10.5 (7 mm) crochet hook for attaching fringe, optional

Getting Started

For the fringe, measure and cut 100 pieces of yarn 12" long and set aside.

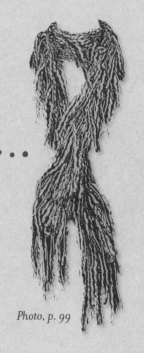

Photo, p. 99

Designed by
Pat Dozier

Submitted by
Weaving Southwest
Taos, NM

Knitting the Scarf

Cast on 12 stitches.

Row 1: *K2, P2; repeat from *.

Repeat Row 1 until you have enough left to bind off. Bind off.

Finishing

Block by pressing with a damp cloth.

Tie 6 pairs of fringe yarn on each end.

Tie remaining fringe by folding in half and tying through knit stitches on the front of the scarf in a staggered pattern.

Scalloped-Edge Hat

Photo, p.112

Designed by
Sarah B. Keller

Submitted by
Knot Another Hat
Hood River, OR

T his cute hat has a garter-stitch border and an oh-so-cute and feminine scalloped edge. Inspiration for the I-cord scallop is from *Knitting Over the Edge,* by Nicky Epstein (Sixth and Spring Books, 2005). Knitted with Cashmerino Super Chunky, it is soft and warm. And oh so fast to knit!

MEASUREMENTS	To fit child (woman) up to 18" in circumference (46 cm) (21" [53.5 cm])
YARN	Debbie Bliss Cashmerino Super Chunky, 55% merino/33% microfiber/12% cashmere, 3.5 oz (100 g)/82 yd (75 m), 16 Yellow
NEEDLES	One US 10.5 (6.5 mm) circular needle 16" (40 cm) long and set of US 10.5 (6.5 mm) double-point needles or size you need to obtain correct gauge
GAUGE	12 stitches and 4.5 rows = 4" (10 cm) in stockinette stitch
OTHER SUPPLIES	Stitch marker, tapestry needle

Knitting the Scallops

Knit 3-stitch I-Cord for 90 (108) rows (see Glossary, page 229).

K3tog onto circular needle.

*Cast on 4 stitches, skip 8 rows I-cord and pick up and knit into next I-cord stitch; repeat from *. You now have 51 (61) stitches.

Place marker at beginning of round.

Knitting the Border

Work circular garter stitch (knit 1 round, purl 1 round) for 3 rounds.

Knitting the Hat

Knit 15 (19) rounds.

Round 16 (20): Knit to last 2 stitches, K2tog. You now have 50 (60) stitches.

Shaping the Crown

Round 1: *K8 (10), K2tog; repeat from *. You now have 45 (55) stitches.

Round 2: *K7 (9), K2tog; repeat from *. You now have 40 (50) stitches.

Round 3: *K6 (8), K2tog; repeat from *. You now have 35 (45) stitches.

Round 4: *K5 (7), K2tog; repeat from *. You now have 30 (40) stitches.

Round 5: *K4 (6), K2tog; repeat from *. You now have 25 (35) stitches.
Change to double-point needles.

Round 6: *K3 (5), K2tog; repeat from *. You now have 20 (30) stitches.

Round 7: *K2 (4), K2tog; repeat from *. You now have 15 (25) stitches.

Round 8: *K1 (3), K2tog; repeat from *. You now have 10 (20) stitches.

For Women's Size Only

Round 9: *K2, K2tog; repeat from *. You now have 15 stitches.

Round 10: *K1, K2tog; repeat from *. You now have 10 stitches.

Cut yarn, leaving a 4" tail. Thread tail onto tapestry needle and thread through remaining 10 stitches. Fasten off on the inside.

Finishing

Weave in ends. Block lightly to shape scallops.

Designed by
Patricia Colloton-Walsh
and Caitlin Walsh

Submitted by
Loop Yarn Shop
Milwaukee, WI

Crocheted Curly Hat

This cute little cap is meant to be unisex, with an optional picot edge for girls. It crochets up so quickly, you'll want to try it in different colors for every baby you know.

SIZES	Infant–6 months
YARN	Noro Blossom, 30% kid mohair/40% wool/20% silk/10% nylon, 1.4 oz (40 g)/77 yds (70 m), 05 Magenta/Purple
NEEDLES	One US J/10 (6 mm) crochet hook or size you need to obtain correct gauge
GAUGE	12–14 stitches = 4" (10 cm) in pattern
ABBREVIATIONS	ch Chain (see Glossary, page 229)
	sc Single crochet (see Glossary, page 234)
	sl st Slip stitch (see Glossary, page 234)

Crocheting the Crown

Row 1: Ch 2, 6 sc in first chain, join last sc to first with slip stitch.

Row 2: Ch 1, 2 sc in every sc of previous row, join last sc to first with slip stitch. You now have 12 stitches.

Making the Curls

Row 3: Ch 1, *3 sc; sc in next sc and chain 12; working back toward base, 3 sc in second chain from hook and in remaining chains to base row. Repeat from * two more times. Join last sc to first with slip stitch. You now have three curls.

Row 4: Ch 1, sc in every stitch and 1 sc in back of curls; join last sc to first with slip stitch. You now have 12 stitches.

Row 5: Ch 1, 2 sc in every stitch; join last sc to first with slip stitch. You now have 24 stitches.

Row 6: Ch 1, sc in every stitch; join last sc to first with slip stitch.

Row 7: Ch 1, *1 sc, 2 sc in next stitch; repeat from *; join last sc to first with slip stitch. You now have 36 stitches.

Row 8: Repeat Row 6.

Row 9: Ch 1, *2 sc, 2 sc in next stitch; repeat from *; join last sc to first with slip stitch. You now have 48 stitches.

Rows 10–12: Repeat Row 6.

Rows 13 and 15: Ch 1, *sc in next 4 stitches, sc dec; repeat from *; join last sc to first with slip stitch.

Rows 14, 16, and 17: Repeat Row 6.

Row 18 (optional picot edge): Ch 1, *3 sc in next stitch, sl st in next stitch; repeat from *.

Finishing

Weave in ends.

Quick & Classy Cabled Clutch . . . .

The inspiration for this clutch came from one that we saw in *InStyle* magazine. We have seen our customers get very creative with their embellishments, and they find this project fun and fashionable!

Photo, p. 98

Designed by
Sarah Marie Fuchs

Submitted by
Bella Filati Luxury Yarns
Southern Pines, NC

MEASUREMENTS	Approximately 10" (25.5 cm) wide and 7" (18 cm) tall
YARN	Ornaghi Filati Country, 50% wool/40% acrylic/10% alpaca, 3.5 oz (100 g)/95 yd (87 m)
NEEDLES	US 11 (8 mm) straight needles or size you need to obtain correct gauge
GAUGE	12 stitches = 4" (10 cm) in pattern

Cable Pattern

The cables are worked over 12 stitches.

C4f = Slip 4 stitches onto cn and hold at front, K4, K4 from cn, K4.

C4b = K4, slip 4 stitches onto cn and hold at back, K4, K4 from cn.

OTHER SUPPLIES 1 yd (1 m) length of ribbon, 1½" (4 cm) wide, purse handles, needle and thread (for ribbon rouching), tapestry needle, cable needle

ABBREVIATIONS cn   Cable needle
C4f   Cable 4 front (see Cable Pattern at left)
C4b   Cable 4 back (see Cable Pattern at left)
M1   Make 1 increase (see Glossary, page 231)

Getting Started

Cast on 39 stitches.

Knitting the First Cables

Rows 1 and 5: P3, K12, P3, K3, P3, K12, P3.

Rows 2, 4, 6, and 8: K3, P12, K3, P3, K3, P12, K3.

Row 3: P3, C4f, K4, P3, K3, P3, C4f, K4, P3.

Row 7: P3, K4, C4b, P3, K3, P3, K4, C4b, P3.

Repeat Rows 1–8 once.

You have finished 2 cable repeats.

Knitting Increase Rows

Row 1: P1, M1, P2, K12, P3, K3, P3, K12, P2, M1, P1. You now have 41 stitches.

Row 2: K2, M1, K2, P12, K3, P3, K3, P12, K2, M1, K2. You now have 43 stitches.

Row 3: P5, C4f, P3, K3, P3, C4f, P5.

Row 4: K5, P12, K3, P3, K3, P12, K5.

Row 5: P5, K12, P3, K3, P3, K12, P5.

Row 6: Repeat Row 4.

Row 7: P5, C4b, P3, K3, p3, C4b, P5.

Row 8: K2, M1, K3, P12, K3, P3, K3, P12, K3, M1, K2. You now have 45 stitches.

You have finished 3 cable repeats.

Knitting Next Cables

Rows 1 and 5: P6, K12, P3, K3, P3, K12, P6.

Rows 2, 4, 6, and 8: K6, P12, K3, P3, K3, P12, K6.

Row 3: P6, C4f, P3, K3, P3, C4f, P6.

Row 7: P6, C4b, P3, K3, P3, C4b, P6.

Repeat Rows 1–8 once.

You have finished 5 cable repeats.

Knitting Decrease Rows

Row 1: P1, P2tog, P3, K12, P3, K3, P3, K12, P3, P2tog, P1. You now have 43 stitches.

Row 2: K3, K2tog, P12, K3, P3, K3, P12, K2tog, K3. You now have 41 stitches.

Row 3: P4, C4f, P3, K3, P3, C4f, P4.

Row 4: K4, P12, K3, P3, K3, P12, K4.

Row 5: P4, K12, P3, K3, P3, K12, P4.

Row 6: Repeat Row 4.

Row 7: P4, C4b, P3, K3, P3, C4b, P4.

Row 8: K2, K2tog, P12, K3, P3, K3, P12, K2tog, K2. You now have 39 stitches.

You have completed 6 cable repeats.

Knitting the Last Cables

Repeat Rows 1–8 of Knitting the First Cables.

Repeat Rows 1–7 of Knitting the First Cables. You have finished 8 cable repeats.

Bind off.

Finishing

Fold edges over purse handles and use yarn to sew securely in place.

Sew side seams to within approximately 2 inches of handles.

Sew ribbon along top edge of one side, ruching the ribbon as you sew it in place.

Weave in ends.

Handle Options

We made handles by cutting wooden dowels to desired length and sanding the edges. You may also purchase round dowel stoppers and glue them to the ends. Paint dowels if you'd like.

Photo, p. 118

Designed by
Linda Morse

Submitted by
String
New York, NY

Cashmere Ski Headband

String's simple pattern for a cashmere headband is suitable for a beginning knitter and lovely enough for all knitters. The cashmere yarn is made especially for String.

MEASUREMENTS	Approximately 19" (48.5 cm) circumference
YARN	String Super Cashmere, 100% cashmere, 1.75 oz (50 g)/58 yds (53 m), 6 Fuchsia (see page 226 for ordering information)
NEEDLES	US 10.5 (6.5 mm) straight needles or size you need to obtain correct gauge
GAUGE	14 stitches = 4" (10 cm) in pattern
OTHER SUPPLIES	Size J/10 (6 mm) crochet hook

Knitting the Headband

Note: Slip stitches purlwise throughout.

Cast on 13 stitches.

Row 1: Slip 1, (K3, P1) two times, K4.

Row 2: Slip 1, K1, P1, (K3, P1) two times, K2.

Repeat Rows 1 and 2 until piece measures 19".

Bind off.

Sew cast-on edge to bind-off edge. Weave in ends.

Crocheting the Flower (optional)

Chain 3, join into a round with a slip stitch.

Round 1: (Sc, ch 3) six times; join to first sc with a slip stitch.

Round 2: (Sc, hdc, 3 dc, hdc, sc) in each ch3 space from round below. Join with a slip stitch.

Cut yarn, weave in ends. Attach flower to band with a safety pin so that it is removable.

Quick Felted Bag..........

W hen we say quick, we mean it! Using size 17 needles, you'll fly right through the knitting. Then just toss the bag into the washing machine to felt and voilà—a perfect little bag.

Photo, p. 120

Photo, p. 120

MEASUREMENTS	11" (28 cm) wide and 9" (23 cm) tall, felted (*Note:* Exact finished measurements will be determined by the yarn and the point at which you stop felting.)
YARN	Brown Sheep Company Burly Spun, 100% wool, 8 oz (227 g)/132 yds (120 m)
NEEDLES	One US 17 (12 mm) circular needle 24" (60 cm) long or size you need to obtain correct gauge
GAUGE	8.5 stitches = 4" (10 cm) in stockinette stitch, prefelted
OTHER SUPPLIES	One snap closure, One decorative button (optional)

Designed by
Sue Coffrin

Submitted by
Adirondack Yarns
Lake Placid, NY

In the Thick of It: Bulky-Weight Yarns

Knitting the Bottom

Cast on 20 stitches.

Work back and forth in garter stitch (knit every row) until piece measures 4" from beginning.

Knitting the Sides

With 20 stitches still on needle, pick up and knit 8 stitches along the end, pick up and knit 20 stitches along long side, pick up and knit 8 stitches along other end. You now have 56 stitches.

Join into a round and work stockinette stitch (knit every round) until piece measures 10" from bottom.

Knitting the Handles

Next Round: K1, bind off 18 stitches, K10, bind off 18 stitches, K9.

Next Round: K1, cast on 24 stitches, K10, cast on 24 stitches, K9. You now have 68 stitches.

Work stockinette stitch for 2". Bind off loosely.

Weave in all ends.

Felting the Bag

Set the washer for the lowest water level, longest washing cycle, and hottest temperature. Place the bag in a pillowcase and pin or tie closed. Add a small amount of mild soap. *Optional:* Wash with a pair of blue jeans to increase agitation. Start the machine and check the bag after one wash cycle. Repeat if more felting is needed.

Mold bag to shape and allow to dry.

Finishing

Sew both sides of snap closure to inside center top of bag. Sew decorative button to the outside over one side of snap.

Filippi Scarf········· · · ·

I f you think the beautiful bulky yarn you saw in the store is just too big for a sweater, go ahead and buy a skein or two anyway. It's perfect for a thin-ribbed scarf like this one, and if you need a last-minute gift, this is it—it knits up lickety-split.

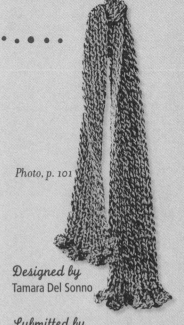

Photo, p. 101

MEASUREMENTS Approximately 4.5" (11.5 cm) wide and 44" (112 cm) long, unstretched

YARN Misti International, Misti Alpaca Chunky, 100% baby alpaca, 1.75 oz (50 g)/108 yds (98 m), 2L474 Yellow

NEEDLES US 13 (9 mm) straight needles or size you need to obtain correct gauge

GAUGE 16 stitches = 4" (10 cm) in rib, unstretched

Designed by
Tamara Del Sonno

Submitted by
Clickity Sticks & Yarns
Minneapolis, MN

Knitting the Beginning Ruffle

Using the knitted-on method (see Glossary, page 231), cast on 64 stitches.

Row 1: *K2tog; repeat from *. You now have 32 stitches.

Row 2: Repeat Row 1. You now have 16 stitches.

Knitting the Body

Row 1: Slip 1 stitch as if to purl, *K1, P1; repeat from * to last stitch, K1.
Repeat Row 1 until scarf is desired length or you have about 25 feet of yarn left.

Knitting the Ending Ruffle

Row 1: Increase in every stitch by knitting and purling into same stitch. You now have 32 stitches.

Row 2: Repeat Row 1. You now have 64 stitches.

Bind off with K2tog method (see Glossary, page 230).

Finishing

Weave in ends.

Designed by
Kerri A. Shank

Submitted by
The Dragonfly Yarn Shop
Janesville, WI

Squashy Bag

This is a bag with personality. The self-striping Noro yarn blends beautifully from one color to the next, and two simple beads add sophisticated embellishment. The bag is held closed with a magnetic clasp.

MEASUREMENTS	Approximately 7.5" (19 cm) wide, 4.5" (11.5 cm) tall, and 4" (10 cm) deep with a 30" (76 cm) strap, felted (*Note:* Exact finished measurements will be determined by the yarn and the point at which you stop felting.)
YARN	Noro Yoroi, 87% wool/7% cotton/6% silk, 3.5 oz (100 g)/131 yds (120 m), Color 4 Purple, Teal, Lime
NEEDLES	One US 11 (8 mm) circular needle 24" (60 cm) long and two US 11 (8 mm) double-point needles for I-cord strap or size you need to obtain correct gauge
GAUGE	Approximately 12 stitches = 4" (10 cm) in stockinette stitch
OTHER SUPPLIES	Stitch markers, magnetic clasp, decorative beads or buttons, 4" (10 cm) of 1" (2.5 cm) grosgrain ribbon for clasp reinforcement, waterproof fabric glue
ABBREVIATIONS	pm Place marker
	sm Slip marker

Knitting the Bag

With circular needle, cast on 21 stitches.

Knit 16 rows.

Knit 21 stitches on needle, pm, pick up and knit 12 stitches along end, pm, pick up and knit 21 stitches along side, pm, pick up and knit 12 stitches along other end, pm (use a marker of a different color to indicate beginning of round). You now have 66 stitches.

Knit in rounds until piece measures 6" from picked-up stitches.

Working the Decrease Rounds

Round 1: K21, sm, K2tog, K8, ssk, sm, K21, sm, K2tog, K8, ssk, sm. You now have 62 stitches.

Rounds 2 and 4: Knit.

Round 3: K21, sm, K2tog, K6, ssk, sm, K21, sm, K2tog, K6, ssk, sm. You now have 58 stitches.

Round 5: K21, purl to end of round.

Knitting the Flap and Reserving Stitches for the Strap

Next Round: K21, bind off 2 stitches, K4 and place on holder, bind off 25 stitches purlwise, K4 and place on holder, bind off 2 stitches. Now 21 stitches remain for flap.

Beginning with right side facing, knit back and forth in stockinette stitch until flap measures 5.5", ending with a right-side (knit) row.

Bind off purlwise.

Knitting the Strap

Place 4 stitches on double-point needle. *K4, slide stitches to other end of needle; repeat from * until strap is 40".

With Kitchener Stitch (see Glossary, page 230), graft to the 4 stitches still on hold.

Felting the Bag

Set washer to lowest water level and hottest temperature; add a small amount of mild soap. Place bag in a pillowcase and tie or pin closed. Run the wash cycle, checking progress every 5 minutes. Reset wash cycle, and stop felting when knit stitches are no longer visible. Rinse well and blot excess water with a towel. Shape and allow to dry.

Finishing

Cut two 2" pieces of grosgrain ribbon. Press ends under so piece measures 1". Cut slits for prongs of snap. Attach male end of snap to one ribbon piece.

Apply female end of snap to bag body 3" from upper edge, using second piece of ribbon for backing on inside of bag.

Line up the snap ends and glue the male end to the underside of the flap. Let the glue dry.

Decorate the flap with beads, buttons, or flowers.

Cozy House Socks

These cozy socks knit up fast and are an easy introduction to sock knitting. Pick a bulky worsted yarn and get busy. You can probably finish a pair this weekend!

Photo, p.105

Designed by
Sue Dial
Harvest Moon Handspun

Submitted by
Baskets of Yarn
Charlotte, NC

MEASUREMENTS	3" (7.5 cm) from top of cuff to top of heel, 9.5" (24 cm) from back of heel to end of toe
YARN	Feza Cypress Mohair, 35% wool/65% acrylic, 3.5 oz (100 g)/198 yds (181 m)
NEEDLES	US 7 (4.5 mm) straight needles and set of US 6 (4 mm) double-point needles or size you need to obtain correct gauge
GAUGE	18 stitches and 24 rows = 4" (10 cm) on larger needle in stockinette stitch
OTHER SUPPLIES	Stitch holder, tapestry needle

Knitting the Cuff

With straight needles, cast on 40 stitches, leaving a 12" tail.

Slipping the first stitch of every row, work K2, P2 ribbing for 16 rows.

Knitting the Heel Flap

Change to double-point needles as follows:

Slip first 10 stitches onto double-point needle.

Slip next 20 stitches onto stitch holder.

Slip last 10 stitches onto a second double-point needle. Yarn tail is at beginning of Needle 1. With WS facing, purl 10 stitches from Needle 3 to Needle 1. You now have 20 stitches on one double-point needle.

Work back and forth as follows.

Row 1: Slip 1, *K1, slip 1; repeat from * to last stitch, K1.

Row 2: Slip 1, purl to end of row.

Repeat Rows 1 and 2 until piece measures 2.5", ending after completing Row 1.

Turning the Heel

Row 1 (wrong side): Slip 1, P11, P2tog, P1, turn.

Row 2: Slip 1, K5, ssk, K1, turn.

Row 3: Slip 1, P6, P2tog, P1, turn.

Row 4: Slip 1, K7, ssk, K1, turn.

Row 5: Slip 1, P8, P2tog, P1, turn.

Row 6: Slip 1, K9, ssk, K1, turn.

Row 7: Slip 1, P10, P2tog, turn.

Row 8: Slip 1, K10, K2tog. Leave these 12 stitches on needle.

Knitting the Heel Gussets

With another double-point needle, pick up and knit 10 stitches along side of heel flap, then slip these 10 stitches onto needle with 12 heel flap stitches. You now have 22 stitches on Needle 1.

With Needle 2, knit 20 stitches from holder.

With Needle 3, pick up and knit 10 stitches along the other edge of the heel flap and knit the first 6 stitches from Needle 1 onto same needle.

You now have 16 stitches on Needle 1, 20 stitches on Needle 2, and 16 stitches on Needle 3. Knit 1 round.

Round 1:

    Needle 1   K to last 3 stitches, K2tog, K1.

    Needle 2   K 20.

    Needle 3   K1, ssk, knit to end of round.

Round 2: Knit.

Repeat Rounds 1 and 2 until there are 10 stitches on Needles 1 and 3 and 20 stitches on Needle 2.

Knitting the Foot

Work stockinette stitch (knit every round) until foot measures 2 inches less than desired finished length.

Shaping the Toe

Round 1:

    Needle 1   Knit to last 3 stitches, K2tog, K1.

    Needle 2   Knit 1, ssk, knit to last 3 stitches, K2tog, K1.

    Needle 3   Knit 1, ssk, knit to end.

Round 2: Knit.

Repeat Rounds 1 and 2 until there are 5 stitches on Needles 1 and 3 and 10 stitches on Needle 2.

Finishing

Graft toe stitches together with Kitchener Stitch (see Glossary, page 230). Thread 12" tail onto tapestry needle, then sew back seam.

Weave in ends. Block.

Short & Sassy Shawl........

Photo, p. 118

This type of shawl has been seen in the Milwaukee area around the waists of dancers before and after practices. It is very versatile, and can be pinned or knotted at the shoulder.

MEASUREMENTS	Approximately 52" (132 cm) wide and 12" (30.5 cm) deep, without fringe
YARN	Noro Iro, 75% wool/25% silk, 3.5 oz (100 g)/131 yds (120 m), Color 54
NEEDLE	One US 19 (15 mm) circular needle 29" (74 cm) long or longer or size you need to obtain correct gauge
GAUGE	8 stitches = 4" (10 cm) in pattern
NOTE	Knit the first stitch of every row a bit looser than usual so the sides do not bind.

Designed by
Patricia Colloton-Walsh and Caitlin Walsh

Submitted by
Loop Yarn Shop
Milwaukee, WI

Getting Started

Measure out and cut 20 yards of yarn to be used for fringe.

Knitting the Shawl

Cast on 4 stitches.

Row 1: Knit.

Row 2 and all following rows: K1, Kfb, knit to last 2 stitches, Kfb, K1.

Continue until you have only enough yarn left to bind off.

Bind off loosely.

Making the Fringe

Cut 50 strands 14" long. Attach single strands evenly spaced, 25 strands on each side of bottom point.

Finishing

Weave in ends.

Designed by
Miriam G. Briggs

Submitted by
Wool Away
St. Johnsbury, VT

Broken Rib Stitch Pattern

Row 1: *K3, P1; repeat from * to last stitch, K1.

Bulky Collar

Here's a fun alternative to the scarf—a buttoned collar that you can wear with a lighter-weight crew neck or even a cotton turtleneck. And it's easy to knit—every row is the same!

MEASUREMENTS	Approximately 16" (40.5 cm) circumference, 5" (12.5 cm) deep with collar folded down
YARN	Bulky: Classic Elite Sinful, 100% cashmere, 1.75 oz (50 g)/65 yds (59 m), 92027 Wisteria
	Super bulky: Classic Elite Forbidden, 100% cashmere, 1.75 oz (50 g)/65 yds (59 m), 10071 Marled Seaglass
NEEDLES	US 13 (9 mm) straight needles for bulky, US 15 (10 mm) straight needles for super bulky, or size you need to obtain correct gauge
GAUGE	12 stitches and 16 rows in bulky, 11 stitches and 16 rows in super bulky = 4" in pattern
OTHER SUPPLIES	1 or 2¾" (2 cm) button(s)

Knitting the Collar

Cast on 25 (21) stitches.

Work Broken Rib Stitch Pattern (see at left) until piece measures 14" from beginning.

Buttonhole Row: Keeping in pattern, bind off the 14th (10th) and the 22nd (18th) stitches.

Bind-off Row: Bind off all stitches in pattern. When you come to a previously bound-off stitch, cast on 1 stitch and bind it off to form a buttonhole.

Finishing

Weave in ends. Sew on buttons.

Knitted Cap with Pigtails

Photo, p. 102

This hat is knitted from yarn that I hand-paint with acid dyes. Each skein has at least three colors or shades. The yarn is put up in 4-ounce skeins, and a single strand works out to 18 stitches per 4 inches on size US 7 needles. For this cap, the yarn is used doubled throughout.

MEASUREMENTS	Approximately 19" (48.5 cm) circumference
YARN	Kaolin Designs RiverStone, 100% merino wool, 4 oz (113 g)/280 yds (256 m) (*Note:* Yarn is used doubled throughout.)
NEEDLES	Set of US 10 (6 mm) double-point needles or size you need to obtain correct gauge
GAUGE	14 stitches = 4" (10 cm) in pattern
OTHER SUPPLIES	One US J/10 (6 mm) crochet hook, tapestry needle

Designed by
Linda O'Leary

Submitted by
Kaolin Designs
Gastonia, NC

Getting Started

Cast on 61 stitches and divide onto three needles. Join into a round, being careful not to twist stitches.

Rounds 1–6: *K1, P1; repeat from *.

Rounds 7–9: Knit.

Rounds 10–12: *K1, P1; repeat from *.

Repeat Rounds 7–12 four more times.

Knit 2 rows even decreasing 1 stitch. You now have 60 stitches.

Decreasing for the Crown

Decrease Round 1: *K2tog, K3; repeat from *. You now have 48 stitches.

Rounds 37–38: Knit.

Round 39: *K2tog, K2; repeat from *. You now have 36 stitches.

Rounds 40–41: Knit.

Round 42: *K2tog, K1; repeat from *. You now have 24 stitches.

Round 43: Knit.

Round 44: *K2tog; repeat from *. You now have 12 stitches.

Break yarn, leaving a 10" tail. Thread tail onto tapestry needle and draw through remaining 12 stitches twice, pull up snug, and fasten off on the inside. Weave in end.

Making the Pigtails

With crochet hook and two strands of yarn, chain 20 stitches.

Work 2 sc in second chain from hook and in each remaining stitch. Do not cut yarn.

*Ch 20, 2 sc in second chain from hook and each remaining stitch. Do not cut yarn. Repeat from * seven more times. You now have 9 pigtails.

Finishing

Gather together the pigtails and fasten to top of hat. Weave in all ends.

Felted Gift Bag

Photo, p. 101

Here is the ultimate in recycling: the infinitely reusable gift bag! They say that good things come in small packages; why not let the package be as good as the contents?

MEASUREMENTS   Approximately 15" (38 cm) around and 5.5" (14 cm) tall (*Note:* Exact finished measurements will be determined by the yarn and the point at which you stop felting.)

YARN   Klippan Mattgarn, 100% wool, 3.5 oz (100 g)/140 yds (128 m), Color 5057

Designed by
Nancy Miller

Submitted by
KnitWit Yarn Shop
Portland, ME

NEEDLES	One US 10 (6 mm) circular needle 16" (40 cm) long and one set of US 10 (6 mm) double-point needles or size you need to obtain correct gauge
GAUGE	Approximately 14 stitches = 4" (10 cm), before felting
OTHER SUPPLIES	½" (1.3 cm) ribbon 18" (46 cm) long, tapestry needle
ABBREVIATIONS	M1 Make 1 increase (see Glossary, page 231)

Knitting the Bag

Cast on 60 stitches. Join into a round, being careful not to twists stitches.

Note: Change to double-point needles when necessary.

Rows 1–4: Knit.

Row 5: *K4, K2tog; repeat from *. You now have 50 stitches.

Row 6: *Yo, K2tog, K3.

Rows 7 and 8: Knit.

Row 9: *K5, M1; repeat from *. You now have 60 stitches.

Knit 28 rows.

Row 38: *K4, K2tog. You now have 50 stitches.

Rows 39–41: Knit.

Row 42: *K3, ssk; repeat from *. You now have 40 stitches.

Rows 43 and 44: Knit.

Row 45: *K2, K2tog; repeat from *. You now have 30 stitches.

Row 46: Knit.

Row 47: *K1, K2tog. You now have 20 stitches.

Row 48: Knit.

Row 48: *K2tog; repeat from *. You now have 10 stitches.

Row 49: Knit.

Row 50: *K2tog; repeat from *. You now have 5 stitches.

Cut yarn, leaving a 10" tail. Thread tail onto tapestry needle and draw yarn through remaining stitches. Pull up snug, fasten off, and weave in end.

Felting the Bag

Set the washing machine for the lowest water level, longest washing cycle, and hottest temperature. Place bag in machine with a pair of jeans or other heavy garment. Start the washer and check the felting progress frequently. It took approximately three agitation cycles to felt to desired size.

Fill the bag with popcorn or beans to shape while drying. Defuzz and thread ribbon through holes.

Stirling Cloche

S artorial historians believe that the cloche was popular with 1920s flappers because of the proud gaze it required of its wearer — chin tilted skyward and eyes peering down the nose. This version features a double strand of a lustrous mohair loop and is slightly felted to fit the wearer.

Photo, p. 115

Designed by
Cirilia Rose

Submitted by
Webs
Northampton, MA

MEASUREMENTS	Approximately 26.5" (67.5 cm) around preshrunk and 22" (56 cm) around shrunk and felted (*Note:* Exact finished measurements will be determined by the yarn and the point at which you stop felting, and you may vary the size of the finished hat by drying it over a form of desired circumference.)
YARN	Valley Yarns Stirling Mohair, 78% mohair/13% wool/9% nylon, 8 oz (227 g)/500 yds (457 m), Bright Taupe
NEEDLES	One US 10 (6 mm) circular needle 16" (40 cm) long and set of US 10 (6 mm) double-point needles or size you need to obtain correct gauge
GAUGE	12 stitches and 16 rows = 4" (10 cm) in stockinette stitch
OTHER SUPPLIES	Tapestry needle. **Optional:** 12" (30.5 cm) of ribbon and one button for trim.

Knitting the Brim

Using two strands of yarn held together, cast on 90 stitches. Place a marker for beginning of round and join, being careful not to twist stitches.

Work even in stockinette stitch (knit every round) until piece measures 2.5" from beginning.

Work two decrease rounds as follows.

Decrease Round 1: *K7, K2tog; repeat from *. You now have 80 stitches.

Next Round: Knit.

Decrease Round 2: *K6, K2tog; repeat from *. You now have 70 stitches.

Knit even until piece measures 5.5" from beginning.

Shaping the Crown

Work decreases for the crown as follows, changing to double-point needles when necessary.

Round 1: *K5, K2tog; repeat from *. You now have 60 stitches.

Rounds 2, 4, 6, 8, and 10: Knit.

Round 3: *K4, K2tog; repeat from *. You now have 50 stitches.

Round 5: *K3, K2tog; repeat from *. You now have 40 stitches.

Round 7: *K2, K2tog; repeat from *. You now have 30 stitches.

Round 9: *K1, K2tog; repeat from *. You now have 20 stitches.

Round 11: *K2tog; repeat from *. You now have 10 stitches.

Cut yarn. With tapestry needle, thread tail through remaining stitches and draw up tight. Fasten off and weave in all ends.

Felting

Wash hat by hand using hot soapy water and vigorous agitation. Squeeze out as much moisture as possible and pull into shape. Allow to dry fully over a bowl or similar form.

Finishing

Embellish as desired.

101

Heavyweight Champs: Heavy Worsted Yarns

Designed by
Karen J. Minott

Submitted by
Webs
Northampton, MA

The Twisted Knee-High Sock

These are terrific warm and stylish socks to wear on cold winter nights or with a jeans skirt. They are so very soft on your feet! The satin bow in the eyelet row gives the pair a whimsical look. The yarn, which is created by Gail Callahan, is available through Webs in Northampton, Massachusetts.

MEASUREMENTS	Approximately 9.5" (24 cm) from top of cuff to top of heel and 8" (20.5 cm) from back of heel to tip of toe
YARN	Kangaroo Dyer, Blueface Leicester, 50% Blueface Leicester/ 50% alpaca, 8 oz (227 g)/350 yd (320 m), Stormy Teal
NEEDLES	Set of US 5 (3.75 mm) double-point needles or size you need to obtain correct gauge
GAUGE	24 stitches = 4" (10 cm) in pattern
OTHER SUPPLIES	30" (76 cm) length of ribbon, ¼–½" (6 mm–1.3 cm) wide
ABBREVIATIONS	LT Left Twist (see Stitch Patterns, facing page)
	RT Right Twist (see Stitch Patterns, facing page)
	tbl through back loop

Knitting the Leg

Cast on 48 stitches. Divide the stitches evenly among three needles (16 on each) and join into a round.

* K1, P1; repeat from * to end of rounds until piece measures 1".

Eyelet Round: * K2tog, yo; repeat from * to end of round.

Next Round: Knit to end of round.

Pattern Round 1: * K1 tbl, 3 Seed Stitch, P2, K3, P2, 3 Seed Stitch, K2 tbl; repeat from * to end of round.

Pattern Round 2: * K1 tbl, 3 Seed Stitch, P2, RT, P2, 3 Seed Stitch, K2 tbl; repeat from * to end of round.

Pattern Round 3: Repeat Round 1.

Pattern Round 4: * K1 tbl, 3 Seed Stitch, P2, LT, P2, 3 Seed Stitch, K2 tbl; repeat from * to end of round.

Repeat Rounds 1–4 until piece measures 8"–9.5", or desired length to top of foot.

Knitting the Heel Flap

In this step, continue to work the established pattern and at the same time redistribute the stitches as follows:

Move the last 4 stitches of Needle 1 to Needle 2. Move the first 5 stitches of Needle 3 to Needle 2. (Needle 1 has 12 stitches, Needle 2 has 25 stitches, and Needle 3 has 11 stitches.)

Knit the 12 stitches on Needle 1 to Needle 3. Turn, purl 1 row. These are the 23 heel flap stitches, and in the next step you will work back and forth on them in rows. Leave the remaining 25 stitches on Needle 2 unworked for now.

Row 1: Slip 1 as if to purl, * K1, slip 1 as if to knit; repeat from * to end of row.

Row 2: Purl to end of row.

Repeat these two rows eight more times.

Repeat Row 1 (19 rows in all).

Turning the Heel

Continue working back and forth on the 23 heel flap stitches, as follows:

(Wrong Side) P13, P2tog, P1, turn.

Slip 1, K4, ssk, K1, turn.

Slip 1, P5, P2tog, P1, turn.

Slip 1, K6, ssk, K1, turn.

Continue in this manner, working one more stitch before the decrease in each row until 13 stitches remain on your needle.

Stitch Patterns

Left Twist (LT): K1, knit second stitch through the back loop, then knit the first stitch through the front and slide both off the needle at the same time.

Right Twist (RT): Knit second stitch on needle without taking the stitch off, then knit the first stitch and slide both off the needle at the same time, K1.

Seed Stitch (3-stitch repeat):
   Round 1: K1, P1, K1;
   Round 2: Purl the knit stitches and knit the purl stitches. Repeat Rounds 1 and 2 for pattern.

Knitting the Gusset

Redistribute the stitches as follows:

Needle 1 With an empty needle, pick up and knit 10 stitches along the left side of the heel flap for Needle 1.

Needle 2 Knit the first 6 stitches that have been on hold for the sock front. Continue in established patterns on the next 13 stitches, K6. You now have 25 stitches on Needle 2.

Needle 3 With an empty needle, pick up and knit 10 stitches along the right side of the heel flap, then knit 6 stitches from the heel flap onto Needle 3. You now have 16 stitches on Needle 3.

Slip the remaining 7 stitches from the heel flap onto Needle 1. You now have 17 stitches on Needle 1.

You now have 58 stitches total. The beginning of each round is at the center back.

Round 1:

Needle 1 Knit to last 3 stitches, K2tog, K1.

Needle 2 Work in established patterns.

Needle 3 K1, ssk, knit to end of needle.

Round 2: Knit to end of round.

Rounds 3–6: Repeat Rounds 1 and 2. You now have 14 stitches on Needle 1, 25 stitches on Needle 2, and 13 stitches on Needle 3.

Round 7:

Needle 1 Knit to last 3 stitches, K2tog, K1.

Needle 2 K1, ssk, work to last 3 stitches, k2tog, k1.

Needle 3 K1, ssk, knit to end of needle.

You now have 48 stitches.

Knitting the Foot

Work in established pattern with no further decreases until the foot measures 2 inches less than the desired length.

Knitting the Toe

From here, you knit on every needle: No more patterning!

Slip 1 stitch from Needle 2 to Needle 3.

Round 1:

    Needle 1 Knit to last 3 stitches, K2 tog, K1.

    Needle 2 K1, ssk, knit to last 3 stitches, K2tog, K1.

    Needle 3 K1, ssk, knit to end of needle.

Round 2: Knit to the end of each needle.

Rounds 3–16: Repeat Rounds 1 and 2. You now have 16 stitches.

Knit 4 stitches from Needle 1 onto Needle 3. Needles 3 and 2 each have 8 stitches.

Finishing

Cut yarn, leaving a 16" tail. Using Kitchener Stitch (see Glossary, page 230), graft the 16 stitches together. Weave in any loose ends.

Weave the ribbon through the eyelets at the top of the ribbing.

Cabled Headband·············

Photo, p. 118

This lovely cabled headband is wonderfully comfortable to wear. It is shaped from 4.5" at its widest point for maximum forehead coverage down to 3" at its narrowest point for maximum comfort at the back of the neck.

MEASUREMENTS	Approximately 21" (53.5 cm) around
YARN	Cascade Pastaza, 50% llama/50% wool, 3.5 oz (100 g)/132 yds (121 m), 002 Natural
NEEDLES	US 7 (4.5 mm) straight needles or size you need to obtain correct gauge
GAUGE	18 stitches = 4" (10 cm) in stockinette stitch

Designed by
Ann Schantz

Submitted by
Grafton Yarn Store
Grafton, WI

Heavyweight Champs: Heavy Worsted Yarns

OTHER SUPPLIES Cable needle, extra needle for bind-off, scrap yarn and crochet hook for cast-on (optional)

Knitting the Headband

Using provisional method (see Glossary, page 223), cast on 18 stitches.

Row 1 (right side): Slip 3 stitches purlwise with yarn in back, P3, K6, P3, K3.

Row 2 (wrong side): Slip 3 stitches purlwise with yarn in front, K3, P6, K3, P3.

Repeat Rows 1 and 2, making Cable Cross (see at left) on center 6 stitches every 8 rows.

Continue in this manner until piece measures 2".

Working the Increases

Increases are worked on right-side rows every 2" by purling in the front and back of the stitch after the beginning slip 3 and before the final knit 3. Work increases when piece measures 2", 4", 6", and 8". You now have 26 stitches.

Maintaining established patterns, work even until piece measures 13" from beginning.

Working the Decreases

Decreases are worked on right-side rows every 2" by purling 2 together after the beginning slip 3 and before the final knit 3. Work decreases when piece measures 13", 15", 17", and 19". You now have 18 stitches.

Maintaining established patterns, work even until piece measures 21" from beginning.

Joining the Seam

Place provisionally cast-on stitches on a needle. Join beginning and end stitches with the three-needle bind-off or Kitchener Stitch (see Glossary, pages 235 and 230).

Finishing

Weave in ends.

Cable Cross

Slip 3 stitches onto cable needle and hold in front, K3, then K3 from cable needle.

Lotus Purse......

T he slip-stitch pattern combined with this particular yarn gives this purse a bit of a woven look. It is elegant but sturdy—the slip stitches produce a dense fabric.

Photo, p. 104

MEASUREMENTS	Approximately 6" (15 cm) wide and 4" (10 cm) tall
YARN	Noro Lotus, 57% rayon/23% nylon/12% acrylic/8% cashmere, 1.75 oz (50 g)/55 yds (50 m), 152 Blue
NEEDLES	US 11 (7 mm) straight needles or size you need to obtain correct gauge
GAUGE	18 stitches = 4" (10 cm) in pattern
OTHER SUPPLIES	One 1" (2.5 cm) button
ABBREVIATIONS	Ssp Slip 1, slip 1, purl two slipped stitches together

Designed by
Tatyana Tchibova

Submitted by
Hilltop Yarn
Seattle, WA

Knitting the Front of the Purse

Note: To work edge stitches, slip the first stitch and purl the last stitch of every row.

Cast on 29 stitches.

Row 1: Sl 1, *K1, Sl 1 wyif; repeat from * to last stitch, P1.

Row 2: Sl 1, *Sl 1 wyib, P1; repeat from * to last stitch, P1.

Repeat Rows 1 and 2 eleven more times (24 rows in total).

Working the Folding Ridge

Row 25: Repeat Row 1.

Row 26: Sl 1, knit to end of row.

Knitting the Back of the Purse

Repeat Rows 1 and 2 seventeen times (34 rows in total).

Knitting the Flap

Decrease Row 1: Sl 1, ssk, *K1, Sl 1 wyif; repeat from * to last 3 stitches, K2tog, P1.

Decrease Row 2: Sl 1, P2tog, *P1, Sl 1 wyib; repeat from * to last 3 stitches, ssp, P1.

Repeat Decrease Rows 1 and 2 until 13 stitches remain.

Working the Buttonhole Rows

Buttonhole Row 1: Sl 1, ssk, K1, Sl 1 wyif, K1, bind off 2, Sl 1 wyif, K1, K2tog, P1.

Buttonhole Row 2: Sl 1, P2tog, P1, Sl 1 wyib, yo twice, P1, Sl 1 wyib, P1, ssp, P1.

Finishing the Flap

Repeat Decrease Rows 1 and 2 until 3 stitches remain. Bind off 3 stitches together: Sl 1, P2tog, psso.

Finishing

Pull the loosest of the 3 bound-off stitches to create a ring at the tip of the flap. Cut three lengths of yarn approximately 6" long and attach them to the ring to make a tassel.

Sew side seams. Weave in ends. Sew on button.

·····The Diotima Shell

Inspired by the look of women's togas in ancient Greece, this super-stretchy, reversible shell will fit women of many shapes and sizes. The shape is hip and so, so easy to knit—not an increase or decrease in sight! The lovely texture of Windsor yarn gives this shell a unique, natural look.

Heavyweight Champs: Heavy Worsted Yarns

Photo, p. 98

Designed by
Kirsten Hipsky

Submitted by
Webs
Northampton, MA

MEASUREMENTS	Approximately 23" (58.5 cm) around and 23" (58.5 cm) long, unstretched; approximately 48" (122 cm) around and 16" (40.5 cm) long, stretched
YARN	Valley Yarns Windsor, 100% unmercerized cotton, 8 oz (227 g)/287 yds (262 m), Spring Green
NEEDLE	One US 15 (10 mm) circular needle 24 or 32" (60 or 80 cm) long or size you need to obtain correct gauge
GAUGE	Approximately 18 stitches = 4" (10 cm) unstretched, approximately 8 stitches = 4" (10 cm) stretched in pattern (K1, P1 rib)
OTHER SUPPLIES	Scrap yarn, tapestry needle

Knitting the Back

Cast on 48 stitches. This cast-on edge will be the shoulder and neck edge of the back. Work 26 rows of K1, P1 rib. Cut working yarn and place stitches on scrap yarn to hold.

Knitting the Front

Pick up first 12 stitches from cast-on edge of back, cast on 24 stitches for the neck opening, pick up last 12 stitches from cast-on edge of back.

Work 26 rows of K1, P1 rib.

At the end of Row 26, place live stitches of front onto left side of needle. Join into a round and work K1, P1 rib on 96 stitches until approximately 7 yards of yarn remain.

Finishing

Bind off loosely in K1, P1 rib. Weave in all ends and block lightly if desired.

Half-and-Half, Please:
Worsted-Mohair Yarns

Photo, p. 100

Designed by
Leanne Walker

Submitted by
KnitWit Yarn Shop
Portland, ME

Wine Gift Bag

With this gift bag, you'll impress your hosts with more than your wine selection! You may want to make one for yourself, too, for your next summertime picnic.

MEASUREMENTS	3.75" (8 cm) at base and 11" (28 cm) tall
YARN	Lang Venezia, 50% mohair/50% acrylic, 1.75 oz (50 g)/141 yd (129 m), Color 0063
NEEDLES	Set of five US 8 (5 mm) double-point needles or size you need to obtain correct gauge
GAUGE	12 stitches = 4" (10 cm) in pattern
OTHER SUPPLIES	US 5/F (4 mm) crochet hook

Knitting the Gift Bag

Begin by making a loop of yarn around thumb. Using the crochet hook, work 8 sc around loop. Tighten loop. Pick up and knit 2 stitches onto each of four needles.

Round 1: Knit.

Round 2: *Kfb; repeat from *. You now have 8 stitches.

Rounds 3–5: Knit.

Round 6: *Kfb; repeat from *. You now have16 stitches.

Rounds 7–11: Knit.

Round 12: *Kfb; repeat from *. You now have 32 stitches.

Check to see if circle is large enough to cover the bottom of the bottle. If not, repeat Rounds 7–12.

Round 13: *Yo, K2tog; repeat from *.

Rounds 14–23: Knit.

Repeat Rounds 13–23 five times, or until desired length.

Drawstring Round: *Yo, K2tog; repeat from *.

Knitting the Ruffle

Rounds 1 and 2: Knit.

Round 3: *Kfb; repeat from *. You now have 64 stitches.

Knit 10 rounds. Bind off loosely.

Making the Drawstring

Crochet a chain 24" long, turn, slip stitch across chain. Cut yarn, weave in ends. Thread the drawstring through the eyelets at the bottom of the ruffle.

Gossamer Shell Scarf······•·····•·

Though lightweight and like a cobweb, this mohair-blend scarf will keep you warm when it is wrapped and tucked under the collar of your coat. When you come in from the cold, untuck and unwrap to reveal a beautiful accessory worn purely for adornment.

Photo, p.104

MEASUREMENTS	Approximately 7" (18 cm) wide and 60" (152.5 cm) long
YARN	Karabella Yarns, Gossamer, 30% mohair/52% nylon/18% polyester, 1.75 oz (50 g)/222 yds (203 m), 6487 Yellow with Gold
NEEDLES	US 5 or 6 (3.75 or 4 mm) or size you need to obtain correct gauge
GAUGE	20 stitches = 4" (10 cm) in pattern

Knitting the Scarf

Cast on 20 stitches. Knit 4 rows. Work in Pattern Stitch (see at right) until piece measures approximately 60". Bind off.

Finishing

Weave in all ends. Block.

Designed by
Tamara Del Sonno

Submitted by
Clickity Sticks & Yarns
Minneapolis, MN

Pattern Stitch

Row 1: K2, (K2tog) twice, *(yo, K1) four times, (K2tog) four times; repeat from * to last 10 stitches, (yo, K1) four times, (K2tog) twice, K2.

Rows 2–4: Knit.

Half-and-Half, Please: Worsted-Mohair Yarns

Photo, p. 118

Designed by
Arlene Graham

Submitted by
Fiberworks
Beavercreek, OH

Lace Pattern

Row 1: K1, *yo, K4, [sl 1, K2tog, psso], K4, yo, K1; repeat from *.

Row 2: Knit.

Repeat Rows 1 and 2 for pattern, slipping the first stitch of each row.

Razor Shell Lace Scarf

H ere is a light and fluffy scarf that is a good showcase for a lightly variegated kid mohair. The lace pattern has just two rows, and only one of those is a pattern row, so you can easily memorize the pattern and knit it up without thinking too much.

MEASUREMENTS	7.5" (19 cm) wide and 48" (122 cm) long
YARN	Crystal Palace Kid Merino, 100% wool, 0.875 oz (25 g)/240 yds (219 m), 9812 Violet
NEEDLES	US 8 (5 mm) straight needles or size you need to obtain correct gauge
GAUGE	Approximately 24 stitches = 4" (10 cm) in pattern
ABBREVIATIONS	Sl 1, K2tog, psso Slip 1 purlwise, knit 2 together, pass slipped stitch over knitted-together stitches and off needle
NOTE	For a neat-looking edge, after the first row slip the first stitch of every row purlwise.

Knitting the Scarf

Cast on 49 stitches.

Knit Lace Pattern (see at left) to desired length or until you're almost out of yarn.

Bind off loosely.

Weave in ends.

Shrug This......

Shrugs are all the rage, and with this loosely knit version (three stitches per inch) you'll be able to "shrug" off the time investment! This shrug is worked from the neck down, and there's no sewing required.

MEASUREMENTS	Approximately 11.5" (29 cm) from bottom rib to shoulder; 30" (76 cm) around
YARN	Rowan Kid Classic, 70% lamb's wool/26% kid mohair/4% nylon, 1.75 (50 g)/153 yds (140 m), 842 Peach
NEEDLES	US 10.5 (6.5 mm) straight needles or size you need to obtain correct gauge
GAUGE	12 stitches = 4" (10 cm) in stockinette stitch
OTHER SUPPLIES	Stitch markers, tapestry needle
NOTE	To create a neat finish to the front edges, slip the first stitch of every row knitwise.

Photo, p. 108

Designed by
Toni Kayser Weiner

Submitted by
Yarn LLC
New Haven, CT

Getting Started

Cast on 53 stitches. Work K1, P1 rib for 3 rows.

Beginning the Raglan Shaping

Set-up Row (wrong side): Slip 1, K2, P6, place marker, P8, place marker, P19, place marker, P8, place marker, P6, K3.

Row 1 (increase row): Slip 1, K2, *knit to marker, yo, slip marker, K1, yo; repeat from * three more times, knit to end. *Note:* Be sure to keep marker just to the right of the single knit stitch between the two yarnovers on every right-side row.

Row 2: Slip 1, K2, purl to last 3 stitches, K3.

Repeat Rows 1 and 2 eleven more times. You now have 32 stitches in sleeve sections.

Finishing the Sleeves

Continue as established for 3 rows, but work sleeve stitches (stitches between the two sets of markers) in K1, P1 rib.

Row 4 (remove markers as you come to them on this row): Slip 1, K2, purl to 1 stitch before marker, bind off in purl this stitch, 32 sleeve stitches, and 1 stitch after marker; purl back stitches to 1 stitch before marker, bind off in purl this stitch, 32 sleeve stitches, and 1 stitch after marker; purl to last 3 stitches, K3.

Finishing the Body and Hem

Row 1 (right side): Slip 1, knit to end.

Row 2: Slip 1, K2, purl to last 3 stitches, K3.

Repeat last 2 rows three more times.

Row 1 (right side): Slip 1, work K1, P1 rib to end.

Row 2: Slip 1, continue in rib as established.

Repeat Row 1.

Finishing

With wrong side facing, bind off loosely in knit. Weave in ends.

Seafoam Shawl ·············

Photo, p. 100

This lacy shawl is quick and easy. It is an excellent pattern for a basic shawl, highly recommended for a beginner. The beaded trim is optional, but worth the effort!

MEASUREMENTS	Approximately 40" (101.5 cm) wide and 22" (56 cm) long
YARN	Rowan Kidsilk Haze, 70% super kid mohair/30% silk, .9 oz (25 g)/229 yds (210 m), 592 Heavenly
NEEDLES	US 9 (5.5 mm) straight needles or size you need to obtain correct gauge
GAUGE	Approximately 12 stitches = 4" (10 cm) in pattern
OTHER SUPPLIES	16 gm large-cut delica beads, beading needle, and nylon thread

Knitting Shawl

Cast on 2 stitches, leaving a tail of approximately 2".

Row 1: K1, yo, K1.

Row 2: Knit.

Row 3: K1, yo, knit to last stitch, yo, K1.

Repeat Rows 2 and 3, leaving enough yarn for two more rows plus bind-off, ending on Row 2.

Next Row: Kfb, *yo, K2tog, repeat from * to last 2 stitches, yo, Kfb, K1.

Knit one row and bind off loosely.

Finishing

Weave in ends. Attach thread to one corner of shawl and, working toward bottom tip, *thread 13 beads, attach thread to fourth yarnover hole; repeat from other corner of shawl.

Designed by
Nancy Miller

Submitted by
KnitWit Yarn Shop
Portland, ME

Half-and-Half, Please: Worsted-Mohair Yarns

For Better or Worsted:
Worsted-Weight Yarns

Eyelet Baby Hat

Designed by
Brigitte Lang

Submitted by
Rainbow Yarn & Fibres
Germantown, TN

This little bonnet is simple, soft, and sweet. You may begin on a circular needle and change to double-point needles when things become too tight, or work on double-point needles for the whole hat.

SIZES	Newborn (3–6 months)
YARN	Rowan Cashsoft DK, 57% wool/33% microfiber/10% cashmere, 1.75 oz (50 g)/142 yds (130 m), 501 Sweet
NEEDLES	One US 6 (4 mm) circular needle 16" (40 cm) long and one set of US 6 (4 mm) double-point needles or size you need to obtain correct gauge
GAUGE	20 stitches = 4" (10 cm) in pattern

Knitting the Band

Using Picot Cast-on (see facing page), cast on 56 (64) stitches.

Knit 4 rows.

Place marker and join into a round, being careful not to twist stitches.

Knit 3 rounds.

Knitting the Eyelet Pattern

Round 1: *K6, yo, K2tog; repeat from *.

Round 2: Knit.

Round 3: K5, *(yo, ssk) two times, K4; repeat from * to last 4 stitches, (yo, K2tog) two times.

Rounds 4–7: Knit.

Rounds 8 and 10: Purl.

Round 9: Knit.

Knitting the Body

Work even in stockinette stitch (knit every round) until piece measures 4¼" (4¾") from beginning.

Knitting the Crown

Change to double-point needles.

Round 1: *K6, K2tog; repeat from *. You now have 49 (56) stitches.

Round 2: Knit.

Round 3: *K5, K2tog; repeat from *. You now have 42 (48) stitches.

Round 4: Knit.

Continue in this manner, working one fewer stitch between decreases and knitting one row even between decrease rounds, until you have 14 (16) stitches.

Next Round: *K2tog; repeat from *. You now have 7 (8) stitches.

Cut yarn, leaving a 10" tail. Thread tail onto tapestry needle, draw through remaining 7 (8) stitches. Pull up snug and fasten off on the inside.

Finishing

Thread cast-on tail onto tapestry needle and sew 4 rows at beginning at bottom edge of hat. Weave in ends.

Meghan's Braids

T his hat will give the young girl in your life something to yodel about! The hat is very comfortable and warm, and the braids not only help keep down the earflaps, but they're downright cute as well.

Picot Cast-on

Using knitted or cable method (see Glossary, page 228), cast on 6 stitches, then bind off 2, leaving 4 stitches. Continue to cast on 6 stitches and bind off 2 until desired number of stitches are on needle.

Photo, p. 103

Designed by
Diana Foster

Submitted by
Lowellmountain Wools
Lowell, VT

For Better or Worsted: Worsted-Weight Yarns

MEASUREMENTS	To fit a child, 18" (45.5 cm) circumference
YARN	Peace Fleece, 70% wool/30% mohair, 4 oz (113 g)/200 yds (183 m), Baghdad Blue
NEEDLES	One US 6 (4 mm) circular needle, 16" (40 cm) long, set of US 6 (4 mm) double-point needles or size you need to obtain correct gauge
GAUGE	18 stitches = 4" (10 cm) in stockinette stitch
OTHER SUPPLIES	Tapestry needle, stitch marker, buttons or beads for embellishment, optional
ABBREVIATION	M1 Make 1 increase (see Glossary, page 231)

Knitting the Earflaps

Wind off 5 yards of yarn for left earflap. Cast on 6 stitches onto a double-point needle. Working back and forth on 2 dpns, knit Rows 1–11 as follows.

Row 1 and all odd-numbered (wrong-side) rows: Purl.

Row 2: K1, M1, K4, M1, K1. You now have 8 stitches.

Row 4: K1, M1, K6, M1, K1. You now have 10 stitches.

Row 6: K1, M1, K8, M1, K1. You now have 12 stitches.

Row 8: K1, M1, K10, M1, K1. You now have 14 stitches.

Row 10: K1, M1, K12, M1, K1. You now have 16 stitches.

Set left earflap aside.

Right Earflap

Working from ball of yarn, cast on 6 stitches onto circular needle.

Work Rows 1–11 as for left earflap. Do not break yarn.

Casting On for the Hat

Beginning with right earflap, still on circular needle, work as follows:

K1, M1, K14, M1, K1; cast on 18 stitches for back of hat; work stitches of left earflap onto circular needle as K1, M1, K14, M1, K1; cast on 30 stitches for front of hat.

Place marker and join into a round, being careful not to twist stitches.

Knitting the Pattern

Work 4-round Stitch Pattern (at right) for 4". On last round, increase 1 stitch. You now have 85 stitches.

Decreasing for the Crown

Change to double-point needles when necessary.

Round 1: *K15, K2tog; repeat from *. You now have 80 stitches.

Round 2 and all even (right-side) rounds through 12: Knit.

Round 3: *K14, K2tog; repeat from *. You now have 75 stitches.

Continue in this manner, working one fewer stitch between decreases and knitting one round even between decrease rounds, through Round 12. You now have 55 stitches.

Round 13: *K9, K2tog; repeat from *. You now have 50 stitches.

Round 14: *K8, K2tog; repeat from *. You now have 45 stitches.

Continue in this manner, decreasing every round, through Round 19. You now have 20 stitches.

Round 20: * K2tog; repeat from *. You now have 10 stitches.

Cut yarn leaving a 10" tail. Thread yarn onto tapestry needle, draw through remaining 10 stitches. Pull up snug, fasten off on the inside. Weave in end.

Making the Braids

Cut 24 strands of yarn 30" long. With tapestry needle, draw two strands through each of the 6 cast-on stitches of both earflaps and pull halfway through—you will have four strands 15" long in each of the cast-on earflap stitches.

Braid loosely with three groups of 8 strands. Tie a double strand of yarn 2" from the end of each braid with a square knot to secure. Trim braids even.

Finishing

Weave in ends. Decorate with buttons or beads.

Stitch Pattern

Round 1: *P1, K1; repeat from *.

Round 2: *K1, P1; repeat from *.

Round 3: Repeat Round 2.

Round 4: Repeat Round 1.

Repeat Rounds 1–4 for pattern.

Photo, p. 98

Designed by
Sarah Marie Fuchs

Submitted by
Bella Filati Luxury Yarns
Southern Pines, NC

Swift Cell Phone Carrier

This is Bella Filati's version of the much needed cell phone case. We have all rifled through our purse trying to locate our ringing phone, only to find it one ring too late. We've added a buttoned strap so you can hook the case onto anything. Our customers add lots of bling.

MEASUREMENTS	Approximately 2.5" (6.5 cm) wide and 4" (10 m) tall with 6" (15 cm) strap (buttoned)
YARN	Berroco Bling-Bling, 60% cotton/38% acrylic/2% aluminum, 1.75 oz (50 g)/92 yd (84 m), 1545 Rust/Gold (*Note:* One skein would make 3 or 4 phone carriers.)
NEEDLES	US 8 (5 mm) straight needles or size you need to obtain correct gauge
GAUGE	17 stitches = 4" (10 cm) in stockinette stitch
OTHER SUPPLIES	One ½" (1.3 cm) button, 5" (12.5 cm) length of grosgrain ribbon, ⅜" (1 cm) wide

Knitting the Carrier

Cast on 24 stitches.

Work in stockinette stitch until piece measures 4" or desired height (depending on size of cell phone), ending with a wrong-side row.

Knitting the Strap

Next Row: Bind off 10 stitches, knit to end of row.

Next Row: Bind off 10 stitches purlwise, purl to end of row.

Work remaining 4 stitches in stockinette stitch (on right-side rows, slip the first stitch purlwise; on wrong-side rows, slip the first stitch knitwise) until strap measures 6" or desired length to buttonhole.

Making the Buttonhole

Row 1: K1, K2tog, yo, K1.

Work 3 rows in stockinette stitch. Bind off.

Finishing

Fold carrier in half and sew side and bottom seams. Whipstitch grosgrain ribbon to inside of strap, from top of carrier to buttonhole. Sew on button. Weave in ends.

Photo, p. 115

One-Skein Scarf · · · · · · · · · · ·

Here's one of those great stitch patterns that look good on both sides, so feel free to let your scarf blow in the wind, knowing you'll always have its best side showing!

Designed by
Bobbe Morris

Submitted by
Haus of Yarn
Nashville, TN

MEASUREMENTS	Approximately 6" (15 cm) wide and 52" (132 cm) long
YARN	Cascade 220, 100% wool, 3.5 oz (100 g)/220 yds (202 m), Color 2446
NEEDLES	US 10 (6 mm) straight needles or size you need to obtain correct gauge
GAUGE	16 stitches = 4" (10 cm) in pattern

Knitting the Scarf

Cast on 27 stitches.

Work K1, P1 rib for 6 rows.

Begin 12-row Stitch Pattern (see at right) and work to desired length or until you have just enough yarn for 6 more rows and bind-off, approximately 3 yards.

Work K1, P1 rib for 6 rows.

Bind off.

Finishing

Weave in ends. Block if desired.

Stitch Pattern

Stitch is worked on a multiple of 6 plus 3 stitches.

Rows 1, 3, and 8: *P3, K3; repeat from * to last 3 stitches, P3.

Rows 2, 7, and 9: *K3, P3; repeat from * to last 3 stitches, K3.

Rows 4, 6, and 11: Knit.

Rows 5, 10, and 12: Purl.

For Better or Worse: Worsted-Weight Yarns

Monica's Flowers

Photo, p. 107

Designed by
Anne Bieter Lenzini

Submitted by
Clickity Sticks & Yarns
Minneapolis, MN

Here's a simple-to-knit flower that you can use to embellish just about anything. Pin it to a hat, to a lapel, or to a scarf. Sew it on a pillow. Make it into a decorative curtain tieback. Attach one to your luggage. You get the picture.

MEASUREMENTS	About 5" (12.5 cm) diameter (*Note:* Exact finished measurements will be determined by the yarn and the point at which you stop felting.)
YARN	For blue flower: Brown Sheep, Handpaint, 85% wool/15% mohair, 1.75 oz (50 g)/88 yds (80 m), Peacock, bit of Limelight, optional
ORANGE FLOWER	South West Trading Company, Amerah, 100% silk, 1.75 oz (50 g)/97 yds (89 m), Citrus
NEEDLES	US 8 (5 mm) straight needles or size you need to obtain correct gauge
GAUGE	14 stitches = 4" (10 cm) (*Note:* Gauge does not have to be exact, but do not knit too loosely or you will have a droopy flower.)
OTHER SUPPLIES	One button of choice; 2" (5 cm) circle of buckram or other stiffener and pin back, tapestry needle (optional)

Knitting the Flower Petals (Make 5)

Cast on 1 stitch.

Row 1: Kfb. You now have 2 stitches.

Row 2: Kfb, K1. You now have 3 stitches.

Row 3: Kfb, K2. You now have 4 stitches.

Continue in this manner, increasing in first stitch and knitting to end of row, until you have 20 stitches.

Next Row: *K2tog; repeat from *. You now have 10 stitches.

Knit 2 rows.

Next Row: *K2tog; repeat from *. You now have 5 stitches.

Place 5 stitches on holder.

For Better or Worsted: Worsted-Weight Yarns

Knitting the Leaves (Make 2, Optional)

Cast on 1. Work as for flower petal until you have 10 stitches.

Next Row: *K2tog; repeat from *. You now have 5 stitches.

Knit 3 rows.

Place 5 stitches on holder.

Assembling the Flower

Thread tapestry needle with 12 inches of yarn. Run yarn through all petal stitches, gather, and fasten off. Join leaves in the same way.

Felting

Set the washer for the lowest water level, longest washing cycle, and hottest temperature. Add the flower and a little soap and start the machine. Check felting progress after agitating 8 minutes and every few minutes thereafter until desired look is achieved. Shape the flower and allow to dry.

Finishing

Attach leaves to back of flower (optional). Sew button to center. Sew in all ends. Attach round of buckram behind flower and sew on pin back.

Smiley Scarf ....

This perky and ruffly scarf can be pinned together at the neck or left to dangle freely. It is knit by casting on all stitches at the neck edge and increasing to the outer edge.

MEASUREMENTS Approximately 3.5" (9 cm) wide and 18" (45.5 cm) at neck

YARN Noro Silk Garden, 45% silk/45% kid mohair/10% lamb's wool, 1.75 oz (50 g)/109 yds (100 m), Color 230

Photo, p. 109

Designed by
Elizabeth Prusiewicz

Submitted by
Knit-Knot Studio
Portland, OR

For Better or Worsted: Worsted-Weight Yarns

NEEDLES US 9 (5.5 mm) straight needles or one circular needle 24" or 32" (60 cm or 80 cm) long or size you need to obtain correct gauge

GAUGE 16 stitches = 4" (10 cm) in pattern

ABBREVIATIONS Inc 1 Increase 1 by knitting directly into the bar between the right and left needles without twisting the new stitch

Knitting the Scarf

Note: The first stitch of every row is slipped knitwise.

Cast on 48 stitches.

Rows 1 and 2: Slip 1, knit to end of row.

Row 3: Slip 1, K1, *Inc 1, K1. You now have 94 stitches.

Row 4: Slip 1, purl to end of row.

Row 5: Slip 1, knit to end of row.

Row 6: Slip 1, purl to end of row.

Row 7: Slip 1, *Inc 1, K2; repeat from * to last stitch, K1. You now have 141 stitches.

Rows 8, 10, 12, 14, 16, and 18: Slip 1, purl to end of row.

Rows 9, 13, 17, 19, and 20: Slip 1, knit to end of row.

Row 11: Slip 1, *Inc 1, K2; repeat from *. You now have 211 stitches.

Row 15: Slip 1, K1, *Inc 1, K2; repeat from * to last stitch, K1. You now have 318 stitches.

Bind off.

Finishing

Weave in ends.

Striped and Scalloped Cap

Noro's Silk Garden yarn subtly and beautifully blends a dozen colors in one dynamite skein. Not only is this cap a colorful wardrobe accessory, it's also a delight to knit as you watch the half-inch stripes come to life. Knit in a mock-cable stitch, the cap's scalloped edge is created by a row of single crochet; the crown is topped off with a sprinkling of French knots, to make use of every bit of the single skein. You'll want to knit this cap in many of the other colorways now available.

Designed by
Gwen Steege
Williamstown, MA

Photo, p. 113

MEASUREMENTS	6.5" (16.5 cm) tall and 20" (51 cm) circumference, slightly stretched
YARN	Noro Silk Garden, 45% silk/45% kid mohair/10% lamb's wool, 1.75 oz (50 g)/109 yds (100 m), Color 87
NEEDLES	One US 6 (4 mm) circular needle 16" (40 cm) long and set of US 6 (4 mm) double-point needle, or size you need to obtain correct gauge
GAUGE	20 stitches = 4" (10 cm) in pattern
OTHER SUPPLIES	US F/5 (4 mm) crochet hook, tapestry needle

Knitting the Cap

Cast on 105 stitches.

Round 1: * Slip 1, K2, psso, P2; repeat from * to end of round. You now have 84 stitches.

Round 2: * K1, yo, K1, P2; repeat from * to end of round. You now have 105 stitches.

Rounds 3 and 4: * K3, P2; repeat from * to end of round.

Repeat Rounds 1–4 until piece measures 5" from cast-on edge. Decrease 1 stitch in the last round. You now have 104 stitches.

French Knot

With yarn threaded on a tapestry needle, bring yarn from wrong side to right side where you want your knot to be. With the tip of the needle close to where the yarn exits the fabric, wrap the yarn around the needle twice. (A)

Hold the thread so the wrap stays on the needle and insert the needle close to where it originally exited but not in the same spot. Pull the yarn to the back to form the knot. (B)

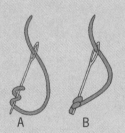

A   B

Decreasing for the Crown

Note: Change to double-point needles when necessary.

Round 1: * K6, K2tog; repeat from * to end of round. You now have 91 stitches.

Rounds 2 and 4: Knit to end of round.

Round 3: * K5, K2tog; repeat from * to end of round. You now have 78 stitches.

Round 5: * K4, K2tog; repeat from * to end of round. You now have 65 stitches.

Round 6, 8, 10, and 12: Purl to end of round.

Round 7: * K3, K2tog; repeat from * to end of round. You now have 52 stitches.

Round 9: * K2, K2tog; repeat from * to end of round. You now have 39 stitches.

Round 11: * K1, K2tog; repeat from * to end of round. You now have 26 stitches.

Round 13: * K2tog; repeat from * to end of round. You now have 13 stitches.

Break yarn, leaving a 12" tail. Thread the yarn through a tapestry needle and draw the yarn through all the stitches on the needle, then draw it through once again, dropping the stitches off the needle and pulling firmly on the yarn to draw the opening closed. Draw the needle to the inside and fasten off the yarn.

Finishing

Join the yarn on the lower edge where the rounds began and ended. Using a crochet hook, *chain 5, skip 4 cast-on stitches, then sc into the next stitch (this is the first "valley" between the mock cables); repeat from * to end of round.

With the remaining yarn, make a series of French knots (see at left) in the crown, centered in the ridge formed by the last purl round.

Aran Tam························

Thisis tam is based on a traditional Aran tam and knitted from yarn produced in Ireland. Originally knitted back and forth and seamed, these instructions have been adapted for knitting in the round.

Photo, p. 116

Designed by
Carol F. Mason Metzger
CFM Designs

Submitted by
My Sister's Knits
Chicago, IL

MEASUREMENTS	Ribbed band about 21" (53.5 cm) circumference after blocking
YARN	Kerry Woollen Mills Aran Wool, 100% wool, 7 oz (200 g)/350 yds (320 m), Bainin
NEEDLES	One US 7 (4.5 mm) circular needle 16" (40 cm) long, set of US 7 (4.5 mm) double-point needles, and US 3 (3.25 mm) straight needles or size you need to obtain correct gauge
GAUGE	28 stitches = 4" (10 cm) in circular stockinette stitch
OTHER SUPPLIES	Cable needle, stitch markers, tapestry needle
ABBREVIATIONS	**(for Cable Stitches, see sidebar on next page).**
	cn Cable needle
	K1b Knit in back of stitch
	Kfb Knit into front and back of stitch

Knitting the Band

With smaller needle, cast on 98 stitches. Work back and forth in twisted rib (K1b, P1) for 6 rows.

Change to larger circular needle but continue working back and forth in rows.

Row 1: *K13, Kfb; repeat from *, placing marker after each increase. You now have 105 stitches.

Row 2 and all even numbered rows: Knit.

Row 3: *K14, Kfb; repeat from *. *Note:* You increase in stitch before each marker and slip marker. You now have 112 stitches.

Rows 5, 7, 9, 11, 13, and 15: Continue in this manner, increasing 7 stitches per row, one before each marker. You now have 154 stitches.

Row 17: *K21, Kfb; repeat from * 6 times, K22. You now have 160 stitches.

Row 18: Knit.

For Better or Worsted: Worsted-Weight Yarns

Cable Stitches

1 Stitch Back Cross (1BC)
Slip 1 stitch onto cn and hold in back, K1, P1 from cn.

1 Stitch Front Cross (1FC)
Slip 1 stitch onto cn and hold in front, P1, K1 from cn.

Knit Back Cross (KBC)
Slip 1 stitch onto cable needle and hold in back, K2, K1 from cn.

Knit Front Cross (KFC)
Slip 2 stitches onto cn and hold in front, K1, K2 from cn.

Purl Back Cross (PBC)
Slip 1 stitch onto cable needle and hold in back, K2, P1 from cn.

Purl Front Cross (PFC)
Slip 2 stitches onto cn and hold in front, P1, K2 from cn.

Right Twist (RT)
K2tog leaving stitches on left needle, knit first stitch again, slip both stitches from needle.

Knitting the Cables

Join into a round. Work in the round from this point beginning with Round 1, following the chart at right or the row-by-row instructions below.

On even-numbered rounds, knit the knits and purl the purls (see Glossary, page 230). Each round consists of five pattern repeats. Change to double-point needles when things get too tight for the circular needle.

Round 1: *RT, P6, KBC, KFC, P6, RT, P1, RT four times, P1; repeat from *.

Round 3: *RT, P5, PBC, RT, PFC, P5, RT, P1, RT four times, P1; repeat from *.

Round 5: *RT, P4, PBC, P1, RT, P1, PFC, P4, RT, P2tog, K1, RT two times, K1, P2tog; repeat from *. You now have 150 stitches.

Round 7: *RT, P3, PBC, P1, 1BC, 1FC, P1, PFC, P3, RT, P2tog, RT two times, K1, P2tog; repeat from *. You now have 140 stitches.

Round 9: *RT, P2, PBC, P1, 1BC, P2, 1FC, P1, PFC, P2, (RT, P2tog) two times; repeat from *. You now have 130 stitches.

Round 11: *RT, P1, PBC, P1, 1BC, P4, 1FC, P1, PFC, P1, RT, p2tog two times; repeat from *. You now have 120 stitches.

Round 13: *RT, P1, PFC, P1, 1FC, P4, 1BC, P1, PBC, P1, RT, P2tog; repeat from *. You now have 115 stitches.

Round 15: *RT, P2tog, PFC, P1, 1FC, P2, 1BC, P1, PBC, P2tog, RT, P1; repeat from *. You now have 105 stitches.

Round 17: *RT, P2tog, PFC, P1, 1FC, 1BC, P1, PBC, P2tog, RT, P1; repeat from *. You now have 95 stitches.

Round 19: *RT, P2tog, PFC, P1, RT, P1, PBC, P2tog, RT, P1 repeat from *. You now have 85 stitches.

Round 21: *RT, P2tog, PFC, RT, PBC, P2tog, RT, P1; repeat from *. You now have 75 stitches.

Round 23: *RT, P2tog, PFC, PBC, P2tog, RT, P1; repeat from *. You now have 65 stitches.

Round 25: *RT, P2tog, 1FC, 1BC, P2tog, RT, P1; repeat from *. You now have 55 stitches.

Round 27: (RT, P2tog) two times, RT, P1; repeat from *. You now have 45 stitches.

Final Decrease Round: *K2tog; repeat from * to last stitch, K1. You now have 23 stitches.

Finishing

Cut yarn, leaving a 12" tail. Thread tail onto tapestry needle, draw through remaining stitches. Pull up snug to close top of hat and fasten off on the inside, leaving tail to sew on pompom. Sew short seam on band and bottom of tam (the parts knit in rows). Make pompom and sew to top of tam. For best fit and appearance, block tam by stretching over tam blocker or dinner plate, misting it with water, and leaving it until dry.

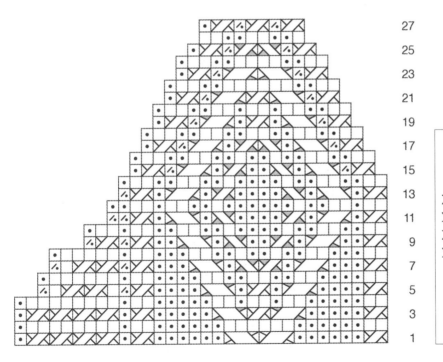

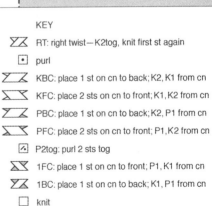

KEY

⧄⧄	RT: right twist—K2tog, knit first st again
•	purl
⧄⧄	KBC: place 1 st on cn to back; K2, K1 from cn
⧄⧄	KFC: place 2 sts on cn to front; K1, K2 from cn
⧄⧄	PBC: place 1 st on cn to back; K2, P1 from cn
⧄⧄	PFC: place 2 sts on cn to front; P1, K2 from cn
⧄	P2tog: purl 2 sts tog
⧄⧄	1FC: place 1 st on cn to front; P1, K1 from cn
⧄⧄	1BC: place 1 st on cn to back; K1, P1 from cn
☐	knit

Be-Ribboned Bonnet

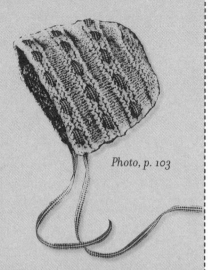

Photo, p. 103

Designed by
Margaret Atkinson

Submitted by
Green Mountain Spinnery
Putney, VT

This bonnet is knitted with Alpaca Elegance, made with Green Mountain Spinnery's baby- and environmentally friendly greenspun process. No petroleum-based products are used in the spinning, and no chemicals are used to bleach, mothproof, shrinkproof, or remove chaff. Bonnet goes with Be-Ribboned Booties (see page 137).

SIZES	Newborn–6 months (6–12 months)
YARN	Green Mountain Spinnery, 50% wool/50% alpaca, 2 oz (57 g)/180 yds (165 m), Natural
NEEDLES	US 6 (4 mm) straight needles or size you need to obtain correct gauge
GAUGE	20 stitches = 4" (10 cm) in stockinette stitch
NOTIONS	2.5 yds (2.25 m) of ¼" (6 mm) ribbon for ties and trim, sewing needle and thread, tapestry needle
ABBREVIATIONS	M1 Make 1 increase (see Glossary, page 231)

Getting Started

Cast on 62 (68) stitches.

Knitting Eyelet Patterns

Rows 1, 2, 3, 5, and 6: Knit.

Row 4: K1, *K2tog, yo, K1; repeat from * to last stitch, K1.

Knit stockinette stitch (knit on right side, purl on wrong side) for 5 rows.

Repeat this 12-row sequence two more times.

Knit in garter stitch (knit every row) until piece measures 4.5" (5.25") from beginning. For smaller size: On last row, (K20, M1) twice, knit to end. You now have 64 stitches. For larger size: On last row, (K14, M1) four times, knit to end. You now have 72 stitches.

Shaping the Crown

Row 1: *K6 (7), K2 tog; repeat from *. You now have 56 (64) stitches.

Row 2 and all even-numbered rows: Knit.

Row 3: *K5 (6), K2tog; repeat from *. You now have 48 (56) stitches.

Row 5: *K4, K2tog; repeat from *. You now have 40 (48) stitches.

Continue in this manner, working one fewer stitch between decreases on each decrease row until 16 stitches remain.

Next Row: *K2tog; repeat from *. You now have 8 stitches

Cut yarn, leaving a 10" tail. Thread yarn onto tapestry needle and draw through remaining 8 stitches. Pull up snugly and secure.

Sew back seam of bonnet from third eyelet pattern to crown for 3" (3.5").

Finishing

Weave in ends.

Wash in warm water with a vegetable-based soap. Roll in a towel, press out excess moisture, lay flat to dry.

Thread 32" ribbon through eyelets closest to cast-on edge for tie. Thread ribbons through next eyelet rows and tack to inside with sewing thread. Be sure to thread ribbons loosely to allow the bonnet to "give" for a comfortable fit.

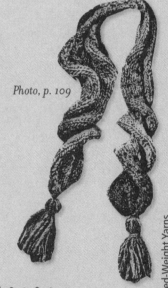

Photo, p. 109

Twisted Spiral Neckscarf······

Here's a delightful new "twist" on the ever-popular scarf. Knitting with short rows makes this scarf cascade from the neck in a spiral, and the graduating color scheme of the yarn makes the design look very well planned.

Designed by
Judy Warde

Submitted by
KnitWit Yarn Shop
Portland, ME

For Better or Worsted: Worsted-Weight Yarns

Working Short Rows

Working a short row means that you work to a certain point in the row (short of the end), then WT, which means wrap the next stitch and turn.

Work the number of stitches specified. Bring the yarn to the front of the work and slip the next stitch from the left needle to the right needle as if to purl. Bring the yarn to the back again and return the slipped stitch to the left needle. Turn. The first stitch on the right needle now has the working yarn wrapped around its base. Continue as instructed.

To hide the wraps, insert the right needle tip under the wrap from front to back and from bottom to top and then into the wrapped stitch as if to knit. Knit the stitch together with its wrap.

MEASUREMENTS	Approximately 2.5" (6.5 cm) wide and 34" (86.5 cm) long
YARN	Noro Kureyon, 100% wool, 1.75 oz (50 g)/91 yds (100 m), Color 92
NEEDLES	US 8 (5 mm) straight needles or size you need to obtain correct gauge
GAUGE	18 stitches = 4" (10 cm) in pattern
ABBREVIATIONS	WT Wrap and turn (See at left.)

Knitting the First Spiral

Cast on 18 stitches.

Set-up Row: Slip 1 Kwise wyib, K8, P9.

Row 1: Slip 1 Kwise wyib, K6, WT, P7.

Row 2: Slip 1 Kwise wyib, K4, WT, P5.

Row 3: Slip 1 Kwise wyib, K2, WT, P3.

Row 4: Slip 1 Kwise wyib, K2, (hide wrap, K1) three times, P9.

Repeat rows 1–4 until the center of the spiral measures approximately 8".

Knitting the Neck

Row 1: K2, P2, K4, P2, K4, P2, K2.

Row 2: P2, K2, P4, K2, P4, K2, P2.

Repeat Rows 1 and 2 until neck section measures 16–18", depending on neck size.

Knitting the Second Spiral

Work Set-up Row and repeat Rows 1–4 until spiral is the same length as first spiral. Bind off.

Finishing

Weave in ends. If you wish, sew closed the small V that is formed at each end of the scarf. If you have a little extra yarn, you can make tassels for the ends. Twist ends into spirals, pin, and block.

Poncho Viva..............

T he poncho trend is alive and well, and this easy-to-knit version in a simple garter drop stitch is sure to please. The stitch is open and airy, and the hand-painted yarn shows it well. Or does the stitch show off the yarn? Either way, it's a winning combination.

Photo, p. 119

Designed by
Cheryl Oberle

Submitted by
Cheryl Oberle Designs
Denver, CO

MEASUREMENTS   Approximately 43" (109 cm) wide and 19" (48.5 cm) long, blocked

YARN   Cheryl Oberle Dancing Colors, 50% merino/50% mohair, 4 oz (113 g)/490 yds (448 m), Red (*Note:* You could get two ponchos out of one skein or make a larger garment.)

NEEDLES   One size US 7 (4.5 mm) circular needle 24" (60 cm) long or size you need to obtain correct gauge

GAUGE   12 stitches = 4" (10 cm) in pattern

Knitting the Poncho

Cast on 130 stitches loosely.

Work Stitch Pattern (see at right) seven times.

Knit 14 rows.

Bind off very loosely.

Finishing

To block, steam or wet the poncho. Lay it out to dry, shaping it to the 43" × 19" measurements.

Fold the blocked poncho in half. Beginning 12" from the fold (or more for an "off-the-shoulder" look) on one side only, sew long edges together on the outside edge.

Stitch Pattern

Rows 1–6: Knit

Row 7: Knit, wrapping yarn around needle three times for each stitch.

Row 8: Knit, dropping extra wraps for each stitch.

Rows 9 and 10: Knit.

Row 11: Repeat Row 7.

Row 12: Repeat Row 8.

For Better or Worsted: Worsted-Weight Yarns

Crocheted Bag

Photo, p. 109

Designed by
Deidra L. Logan

Submitted by
KnitWit Yarn Shop
Portland, ME

This handy bag is quick to crochet, and with all the colors available in Cascade 220, you may want several to coordinate with your wardrobe. The double drawstring pulls the top closed tight to keep the contents of the bag where they belong, inside!

MEASUREMENTS Approximately 4.5" (11.5 cm) diameter at the base and 8" (20.5 cm) tall

YARN Cascade 220, 100% wool, 3.5 oz (100 g)/220 yds (201 m), Color 9436

NEEDLE One US F/5 (4 mm) crochet hook or size you need to obtain correct gauge

GAUGE 19 stitches = 4" (10 cm) in pattern

ABBREVIATIONS ch   Chain (see Glossary, page 229)
dc   Double crochet (see Glossary, page 229)
sl st   Slip stitch (see Glossary, page 234)

NOTES Ch 3 at the beginning of a round creates the first double crochet of the round. "Next stitch" refers to the second stitch of the row to be worked.

Crocheting the Base

Ch 4, join to first chain with slip stitch to form a ring.

Round 1: Ch 3, 11 dc in ring. Join to top of ch3 with slip stitch. You now have 12 stitches.

Round 2: Ch 3, 1 dc in next stitch, 2 dc in each remaining stitch. Join to top of ch3 with slip stitch. You now have 24 stitches.

Round 3: Ch 3, *2 dc in next stitch, 1 dc in next stitch; repeat from *. Join to top of ch3 with slip stitch. You now have 36 stitches.

Round 4: Ch 3, *1 dc in next stitch, 2 dc in next stitch, 1 dc in next stitch; repeat from *. Join to top of ch3 with slip stitch. You now have 48 stitches.

Round 5: Ch 3, *1 dc in next 2 stitches, 2 dc in next stitch, 1 dc in next stitch; repeat from *. Join to top of ch3 with slip stitch. You now have 60 stitches.

Crocheting the Body

Ch 3, 1 dc into the back loop of next 59 stitches. Join to top of ch3 with slip stitch.

*Ch 3, 1 dc in next 59 stitches. Join to top of ch3 with slip stitch.

Repeat from * until bag measures 7" or desired height.

Crocheting the Top

Drawstring Row: Ch 3, 1 dc in next 2 stitches, ch 2, skip 2, *1 dc in each of next 3 stitches, ch 2, skip 2; repeat from *.

Scallop Row: *Ch 1 in the first ch2 space, work 3 dc, ch 1, 3 dc; repeat from *. Slip stitch to first sc to anchor and pull yarn through to finish. You have 12 scallops.

Making the Drawstrings

Measure and cut four lengths of yarn at least 4 yards long. Place two strands side by side, leaving one end 6" longer than the other. Leaving a 2" tail, place a slip knot on the hook and chain along the longer end. At 4", join second strand and, working with yarn double, make a chain of desired length. When double yarn ends, place last loop on holder.

Weaving in the Drawstrings

First drawstring: Starting at center back of the bag and beginning at slip knot end of chain, weave the drawstring into the first space, *behind a group of 3 dc, out the next space, in front of the next group of 3 dc, into the next space; repeat from *. Insert hook into held chain and work slip stitch across the beginning sc chain. Leave 2" tail. Pull tail through last chain.

Second drawstring: Repeat as for first chain starting to weave the chain behind 3 dc (to the right of the first space) and out of the first space, *in front of the group of 3 dc and into the next space, in back of the next group of 3 dc and out of the next space; repeat from *. Insert hook into held chain and work slip stitch across the beginning sc chain. Leave 2" tail. Pull tail through last chain.

Finishing

Weave in ends.

Photo, p. 97

Designed by
Jenny Willey

Submitted by
Clickity Sticks & Yarns
Minneapolis, MN

Decrease

Wrap yarn, draw up loop, wrap yarn, draw loop through first 2 loops on hook but not through last 2 loops on hook; wrap yarn and draw up loop in next stitch to begin second dc, draw loop through first 2 loops on hook but not through last 2 loops on hook (there are 3 loops on hook); wrap yarn and draw up loop in third stitch to begin third dc, wrap yarn, draw loop through first 2 loops on hook, wrap yarn, draw loop through all 4 loops on hook—3 dc have become 1 dc.

Wavy Hat

This cleverly crafted cap is a perfect showcase for this variegated yarn. Though the colors are gradually blending from one to the next, the end result is a series of almost perfect stripes. Crocheted in the round, the waves are formed by increasing and decreasing.

MEASUREMENTS Approximately 19" (50 cm) circumference, unstretched

YARN South West Trading Company, Karaoke, 50% wool/50% soy, 1.75 oz (50 g)/109 yds (100 m)

NEEDLE Size G/6 (4.5 mm) crochet hook or size you need to obtain correct gauge

GAUGE 18 dc = 4" (10 cm) in pattern

Crocheting the Hat

Ch 79, sl st in first chain to form a ring. Ch 3, 2 dc in next chain (first increase), *dc in next 6 chains, decrease (see at left), dc in next 6 chains, increase; repeat from *.

Repeat for 14 rounds.

Finishing

To join the top of the hat, hold tips together at decrease points and sc edges together from the center of the hat out, then slip stitch back to center; repeat over next tip until all edges are joined. Fasten off on the inside and weave in ends.

Make two small tassels (see Glossary, page 235) and attach to top center.

Ice Scraper Mitt ··············

If you live in a cold, snowy climate, you already know what a wonderful idea this mitt is. No more snow up the sleeve of your coat! Simply slip your hand inside, grasp the plastic handle, and scrape away while staying dry and warm.

Photo, p. 105

MEASUREMENTS	5" (12.5 cm) wide and 9.5" (24 cm) long
YARN	Peace Fleece, 70% wool/30% mohair, 4 oz (113 g)/200 yds (183 m), Latvian Lavender or Samantha-Katya Pink
NEEDLES	Set of US 7 (4.5) double-point needles or size you need to obtain correct gauge
GAUGE	16 stitches = 4" (10 cm) in pattern
OTHER SUPPLIES	Tapestry needle, stitch marker, five buttons ½", ice scraper
ABBREVIATIONS	K1b Knit 1 stitch through the back loop
	M1 Make 1 increase (see Glossary, page 231)

Designed by
Diana Foster

Submitted by
Lowellmountain Wools
Lowell, VT

Knitting the Inside of the Mitt

Using invisible method (see Glossary, page 229), cast on 18 stitches. Divide evenly onto three needles. Place a marker and join into a round, being careful not to twist stitches.

Round 1: *K3, M1; repeat from *. You now have 24 stitches.

Round 2: *K4, M1; repeat from *. You now have 30 stitches.

Continue to increase on each round as above, having one more stitch between increases until there are 42 stitches on the needles. Work even until piece measures 8.25" from beginning.

Making the Eyelets

Eyelet Round: *Yo, K2tog; repeat from *.

Knit stockinette stitch for 1".

Knitting the Body of the Mitt

Work Pattern Stitch (see at right) for 7.25".

Pattern Stitch

Round 1: *P1, K1; repeat from *.

Round 2: *K1, P1; repeat from *.

Round 3: Repeat Round 2.

Round 4: Repeat Round 1.

Repeat Rounds 1–4 for pattern.

For Better or Worsted: Worsted-Weight Yarns

83

Tapering the Mitt

Decrease to the end of the mitt as follows.

Round 1: *K5, K2tog; repeat from *. You now have 36 stitches.

Round 2: *K4, K2tog; repeat from *. You now have 30 stitches.

Round 3: *K3, K2tog; repeat from *. You now have 24 stitches.

Round 4: *K2, K2tog; repeat from *. You now have 18 stitches.

Finishing

Slip Inside of Mitt to inside and with wrong sides together, pick up and knit together one stitch from outside of mitt and one stitch from provisional cast-on—18 stitches. Work stockinette stitch cuff for 1". Bind off. Remove scrap yarn.

Weave in ends. Sew on buttons. Insert scraper.

Spa Set

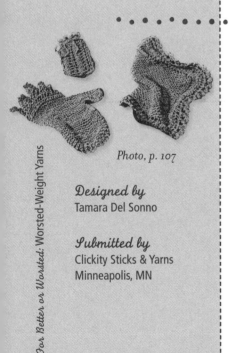

Knitted of soft and drapey bamboo yarn, this set is as luxurious as it is practical. Now all you need is the steam room, the whirlpool, and the massage therapist. Go ahead, indulge yourself!

Photo, p. 107

Designed by
Tamara Del Sonno

Submitted by
Clickity Sticks & Yarns
Minneapolis, MN

MEASUREMENTS	**Facecloth:** Approximately 11" (28 cm) square
	Bath Mitt: Approximately 7.5" (19 cm) long without trim, 8" (20.5 cm) around
	Soap Pocket: Approximately 3.25" (8 cm) × 5" (12.5 cm)
YARN	South West Trading Company, Bamboo, 100% bamboo, 3.5 oz (100 g)/250 yds (229 m), Butter
NEEDLES	Size US 4 or 5 (3.5 or 3.75 mm) straight needles or size you need to obtain correct gauge

Facecloth

Getting Started

Note: Facecloth starts in one corner and is knitted diagonally across the square.

Cast on 5 stitches.

Row 1 (Increase Row): K2, yo, knit to end of row.

Repeat Row 1 until there are 50 stitches.

Row 2 (Decrease Row): K2, yo, K2tog, knit to last 5 stitches, K2tog, K3.

Repeat Row 2 until there are 5 stitches. Bind off.

Knitting the Lace Trim

Cast on 7 stitches and knit 1 row.

Begin attaching lace edge halfway along one long edge. To attach lace as you knit, knit the last stitch of even-numbered rows together with the next garter bump on the edge of the cloth. When you get to a corner, work Rows 2 and 4 into the same edge stitch, then work Rows 2 and 4 into the next edge stitch. Repeat three more times, once in each corner.

Row 1: K1, K2tog, (yo) twice, K2tog, (yo) twice, K2. You now have 9 stitches.

Row 2: K2, (K1, P1 into double yo), K1, (K1, P1 into double yo), K2.

Row 3: K1, K2tog, (yo) twice, K2tog, K4.

Row 4: Bind off 2, K2, (K1, P1 into double yo), K2. You now have 7 stitches.

Repeat Rows 1–4 for pattern.

Finishing

Sew beginning and end of lace stitches together.

Weave in ends.

Bath Mitt

Getting Started

Cast on 60 stitches.

Knit 18 rows.

Bind off 10 stitches at the beginning of the next 2 rows. You now have 40 stitches.

Knit even until piece measures 7" from cast-on edge.

Next Row: *K2tog; repeat from *.

Next Row: Knit.

Repeat these last 2 rows once.

Cut yarn, leaving a 20" tail. Thread tail onto tapestry needle, run tail through remaining stitches twice.

Use remaining tail to sew down along side of mitt and across top of thumb. Gather 9 garter rows around end of thumb and draw tail through these 9 stitches twice. Secure firmly.

Sew along bottom of thumb.

Knitting the Lace Trim

Cast on 6 stitches.

Row 1: Sl 1 wyb, K1, yo, K2tog, yo, K2. You now have 7 stitches.

Row 2: K2, yo, K2, yo, K2tog, K1. You now have 8 stitches.

Row 3: Sl 1 wyb, K1, yo, K2tog, K2, yo, K2. You now have 9 stitches.

Row 4: K2, yo, K4, yo, K2tog, K1. You now have 10 stitches.

Row 5: Sl 1 wyb, K1, yo, K2tog, K4, yo, K2. You now have 11 stitches.

Row 6: K2, yo, K6, yo, K2tog, K1. You now have 12 stitches.

Row 7: Sl 1 wyb, K1, yo, K2tog, K6, yo, K2. You now have 13 stitches.

Row 8: Bind off 7, K2, yo, K2tog, K1. You now have 6 stitches.

Repeat Rows 1–8 to length necessary to go around bottom of mitt. Bind off.

Finishing

Sew lace to edge of mitt and join the ends.

Weave in ends.

Soap Pocket

Getting Started

Cast on 73 stitches.

Picot Edge Row: *K2, increase 1 with backward loop cast-on (see Glossary, page 228), bind off 5; repeat from * to last 2 stitches, K2. You now have 32 stitches.

Knit 2 rows.

Eyelet Row: K3, *K2tog, yo, K4; repeat from * to last 2 stitches, K2.

Knit 2 rows.

Knitting the Body

Row 1: Knit.

Row 2: *K1, yo, P1, P3tog, P1, yo; repeat from * to last 2 stitches, K2. Repeat Rows 1 and 2 until piece measures 4–5".

Bind off, sew across bottom and down side.

Finishing

Weave in all ends. Make a crochet chain 12–15" long. Run chain through eyelet row, tie knots in ends, and use to tie pocket closed to secure soap.

Photo, p. 101

Designed by
Pat Corr

Submitted by
Whitmore Lake Yarn
Company
Whitmore Lake, MI

This 'n' That Hat

For this baby/toddler hat, I've combined my favorite kid-let features—rolled edge, relaxed ribbing, cutesy tassel. This hat is a great way to show your expertise or practice new stitch combinations.

MEASUREMENTS	Baby/toddler, approximately 14" (35.5 cm) around
YARN	Plymouth Encore, 75% acrylic/25% wool, 3.5 oz (100 g)/200 yds (183 m), 241 Pink
NEEDLES	One US 7 (4.5 mm) circular needle 16" (40 cm) long and set of US 7 (4.5 mm) double-point needles or size you need to obtain correct gauge
GAUGE	20 stitches = 4" (10 cm) in pattern
OTHER SUPPLIES	Stitch markers, tapestry needle

Knitting the Band

Cast on 72 stitches loosely. If using double-point needles throughout, divide stitches so there are 24 stitches on each of three needles. Place marker and join into a round, being careful not to twist stitches.

Knit 4 rounds.

Work K3, P1 rib for 1". On last round, place marker every 12 stitches.

Knitting the Pattern Sequence

The hat is set up in six groups of 12 stitches each.

Rounds 1 and 3: *K3, P3, K3, P3, slip marker, (K1, P1) six times, slip marker; repeat from *.

Rounds 2 and 4: *K3, P3, K3, P3, slip marker, (P1, K1) six times, slip marker; repeat from *.

Rounds 5 and 7: *P3, K3, P3, K3, slip marker, (K1, P1) six times, slip marker; repeat from *.

Rounds 6 and 8: *P3, K3, P3, K3, slip marker, (P1, K1) six times, slip marker; repeat from *.

For Better or Worsted: Worsted-Weight Yarns

Rounds 9–16: Repeat Rounds 1–8.

Rounds 17–24: Repeat Rounds 1–8.

Rounds 25–28: Repeat Rounds 1–4.

Rounds 29–32: *K3, P1; repeat from *.

Knitting the Crown

Change to double-point needles.

Round 33: Purl.

Round 34: *P4, P2tog; repeat from *. You now have 60 stitches.

Rounds 35–36: Purl.

Round 37: *P3, P2tog; repeat from *. You now have 48 stitches.

Round 38: Purl.

Round 39: *P2, P2tog; repeat from *. You now have 36 stitches.

Round 40: Purl.

Round 41: *P1, P2tog; repeat from *. You now have 24 stitches.

Round 42: *P2tog; repeat from *. You now have 12 stitches.

Round 43: Repeat Round 42. You now have 6 stitches.

Knitting the Top Ring

Round 1: *Kfb; repeat from *. You now have 12 stitches.

Round 2: Repeat Round 1. You now have 24 stitches.

Round 3–7: Knit.

Bind off loosely.

Finishing

Weave in ends. Add your favorite tassel. Cut eight strands of yarn 18" long. Knot ends, leaving a 1" tail. Work a 3-2-3–strand braid for 8". Tie knot in end and tie around top of hat.

Jamaica Pouch

*Photo,
p. 111*

Designed by
Sandra Clockedile

Submitted by
Webs
Northampton, MA

This handsome drawstring purse is knit in a spiral pattern that accentuates the self-striping yarn. Once you get into the rhythm, this bag works up fast; and no one but you will know how easy it was to knit!

MEASUREMENTS Approximately 6.5" (16.5 cm) around and 7.5" (19 cm) tall

YARN Katia, Jamaica, 100% cotton, 100 g (3.5 oz)/219 yds (200 m), Color 4010

NEEDLES Set of US 6 (4 mm) double-point needles 8" (20 cm) long or longer and one US 6 (4 mm) circular needle 16" (40 cm) long (optional) or size you need to obtain correct gauge

GAUGE 28 stitches = 4" (10 cm) in pattern

OTHER SUPPLIES One crochet hook size F/5 (4 mm), ¼ yd fabric for lining, optional

Knitting the Base

Cast on 6 stitches tightly and place 2 on each of three double-point needles. Place marker and join into a round, being careful not to twist stitches.

Round 1: *Kfb; repeat from *. You now have 12 stitches.

Round 2: *K1, Kfb; repeat from *. You now have 18 stitches.

Round 3: *K2, Kfb; repeat from *. You now have 24 stitches.

Round 4: *K3, Kfb; repeat from *. You now have 30 stitches.

Round 5: *K4, Kfb; repeat from *. You now have 36 stitches.

Round 6: *K5, Kfb; repeat from *. You now have 42 stitches.

Round 7: *K6, Kfb; repeat from *. You now have 48 stitches.

Continue in this manner, adding one knit stitch between increases in each round until you have 126 stitches.

Next Round: Knit.

Next Round: Purl.

Knitting the Pouch Sides

Begin Circular Spiral Stitch (see at right) and continue even until piece measures 6.5" (16.5 cm) from purl row.

Knitting the Top of the Pouch

Next Round: Knit

Next Round: *K2, yo, K1; repeat from *.

Knit 4 rounds.

Bind off loosely.

Finishing

With crochet hook, make two 20–28" (51–71 cm) chains. Thread through holes formed by yarnovers at top of pouch, beginning and ending each drawstring on opposite sides of the bag. Tie ends of drawstrings.

Line if desired.

Circular Spiral Stitch

Round 1: *K2, yo, k2, k2tog; repeat from *.
Repeat Round 1 for pattern.

Fingerless Mittens · · · · · · · · · ·

Fingerless mittens are very handy for anyone who works in the cold, and these two show what a difference the yarn makes! The angora version is quite luxurious and feminine; the alpaca version is just as luxurious in feel but more utilitarian in looks. Both are comfy and warm. The two mitts are worked the same way, but at a different gauge and on different-size needles.

Photo, p. 111

Designed by
Sue Coffrin

Submitted by
Adirondack Yarns
Lake Placid, NY

For Better or Worsted: Worsted-Weight Yarns

Angora Mittens

MEASUREMENTS   Approximately 7.5" (19 cm) long and 8.5" (21.5 cm) around above cuff

YARN   Anny Blatt Angora Super, 70% angora/30% wool, .8 oz (25 g)/116 yd (106 m), 454 Crimson

NEEDLES   Set of US 5 (3.75 mm) double-point needles or size you need to obtain correct gauge

GAUGE   20 stitches = 4" (10 cm) in stockinette stitch

Alpaca Mittens

MEASUREMENTS   Approximately 7" (18 cm) long and 8.5" (21.5 cm) around above cuff

YARN   Catalina Baby Alpaca Chunky, 100% baby alpaca, 3.5 oz (100 g)/ 109 yds (100 m), 105 Lavender Melange

NEEDLES   Set of US 7 (4.5 mm) double-point needles or size you need to obtain correct gauge

GAUGE   18 stitches = 4" (10 cm) in stockinette stitch

Knitting the Cuff (both versions)

Cast on 32 stitches. Divide onto three needles.

Needle 1 12 stitches

Needle 2 12 stitches

Needle 3   8 stitches

Join into a round, being careful not to twist stitches.

Work K1, P1 rib until piece measures 3.5".

Knit 5 rounds.

Shaping the Gusset

Increase Round 1: Kfb in first 2 stitches, knit to end of round. You now have 34 stitches.

Knit 3 rounds.

Increase Round 2: Kfb, K2, Kfb, knit to end of round. You now have 36 stitches.

Knit 3 rounds.

Increase Round 3: Kfb, K4, Kfb, knit to end of round. You now have 38 stitches.

Knit 3 rounds.

Increase Round 4: Kfb, K6, Kfb, knit to end of round. You now have 40 stitches.

Knit 1 round.

Dividing for the Thumb

Place first 10 stitches on holder for thumb.

Cast on 4, join, knit to end of round. You now have 34 stitches.

Knit 2 rounds.

Work K1, P1 rib for 3 rounds.

Bind off in rib pattern.

Knitting the Thumb

Divide thumb stitches onto two double-point needles, 5 stitches on each needle.

Join yarn and knit the 10 stitches.

With third needle, pick up and knit 6 stitches: the 4 cast-on stitches and 1 extra before and after. You now have 16 stitches.

Join into a round, knit 10 stitches.

K2tog, K2, K2tog. You now have 14 stitches.

Work K1, P1 rib for 2 rounds.

Bind off in rib pattern.

Finishing

Weave in ends.

Baby Gnome Hat

Photo, p. 111

Designed by
Sue Dial
Harvest Moon Handspun

Submitted by
Baskets of Yarn
Charlotte, NC

This sweet, easy hat will keep your favorite gnome and his ears warm and toasty all winter long. And he'll look so cute in it!

MEASUREMENTS	Approximately 16" (40.5 cm) circumference
YARN	Harvest Moon Handspun Superwash Merino, 100% wool, 2 oz (56 g)/100 yds (91 m), 7 wpi
NEEDLES	One US 10 (6 mm) circular needle 16" (40 cm) long and set of US 10 (6 mm) double-point needles or size you need to obtain correct gauge
GAUGE	15 stitches and 24 rows = 4" (10 cm) in stockinette stitch
OTHER SUPPLIES	Marker, holder, tapestry needle, size J/10 (6 mm) crochet hook

Knitting the Earflaps

Knit the earflap back and forth on two double-point needles.

Right Earflap

Row 1: Leaving a 2" tail, make a slipknot and put it on a needle. Knit in front and back (Kfb) of this stitch. You now have 2 stitches.

Row 2: Purl.

Row 3: Kfb in both stitches. You now have 4 stitches.

Row 4: Purl.

Row 5: Kfb, knit to last stitch, Kfb.

Repeat Rows 4 and 5 until you have 10 stitches.

Continue in stockinette stitch (knit on right side, purl on wrong side) for 7 more rows, ending having completed a purl row.

Break yarn and place earflap on holder.

Make left earflap but do not break yarn or put stitches on holder.

Beginning the Hat

With circular needle, knit 10 stitches of second earflap, cast on 25 stitches with backward-loop method (see Glossary, page 228), knit 10 stitches of first earflap from holder, cast on 15 stitches. You now have 60 stitches on the circular needle.

Place marker and join into a round, being careful not to twist stitches.

Work in stockinette stitch (knit every round) for 20 rounds.

Shaping the Top

Round 1: *K8, K2tog; repeat from *. You now have 54 stitches.

Rounds 2–4: Knit.

Round 5: *K7, K2tog; repeat from *. You now have 48 stitches.

Rounds 6–8: Knit.

Continue in this manner, decreasing 6 stitches every fourth round, until 6 stitches remain. Break yarn, leaving a 10" tail. Thread tail onto tapestry needle and draw through 6 remaining stitches. Pull up snug and fasten off on the inside. Make a tassel (see Glossary, page 234) and attach to top of hat.

Crocheting the Edges

Starting at tip of right earflap and leaving a 2" tail, work single crochet along one edge of flap, across front of hat, and down front of left earflap. Break yarn, leaving a 2" tail. With new piece of yarn, leave a 2" tail and work single crochet along remaining edge of flap, across back of hat, and down back of right earflap. Break yarn, leaving a 2" tail.

Finishing

Tie three tails together at tips of earflaps.

Weave in ends.

Designed by
Bobbe Morris

Submitted by
Haus of Yarn
Nashville, TN

Stitch Pattern

Rounds 1–3: *P3, K3; repeat from *.

Rounds 4–6: Purl.

Rounds 7–9: *K3, P3; repeat from *.

Rounds 10–12: Knit. Repeat Rounds 1–12 for pattern.

For Better or Worsted: Worsted-Weight Yarns

Scrunchie Hat

The pattern in this hat is very pronounced, with the ridges standing far away from the background. It looks great, and also makes the hat very comfortable to wear. Its cord can be adjusted for a custom fit.

MEASUREMENTS Approximately 22" (56 cm) circumference

YARN Cascade 220, 100% wool, 3.5 oz (100 g)/220 yds (202 m), Color 2446

NEEDLES One US 8 (5 mm) circular needle 16" (40 cm) long and set of US 8 (5 mm) double-point needles or size you need to obtain correct gauge

GAUGE 16 stitches = 4" (10 cm) in pattern

Getting Started

With circular needle, cast on 90 stitches. Place marker and join into a round, being careful not to twist stitches.

Knit 10 rounds.

Work 12-round Stitch Pattern (see at left) four times. Work Rounds 1–11 one more time.

Next Round: *K3tog; repeat from *. You now have 30 stitches.

Decreasing for the Top

Change to double-point needles and purl 2 rounds.

Round 1: *P2tog; repeat from *. You now have 15 stitches.

Round 2: Purl.

Round 3: P1, *P2tog; repeat from *. You now have 8 stitches.

Break yarn, leaving a 10" tail. Thread tail onto tapestry needle and draw through remaining stitches. Pull up snug and fasten off.

Finishing

With two double-point needles, work 4-stitch I-cord (see Glossary, page 229). Tack center of I-cord to center back and tie in front.

Weave in ends.

Picture This! 101

A Tea Cozy, page 128

B Wavy Hat, page 82

C One-Skein-Wonder Baby Sweater, page 11

D One-Car-Ride Coaster Set, page 8

101

A **C**

B **D**

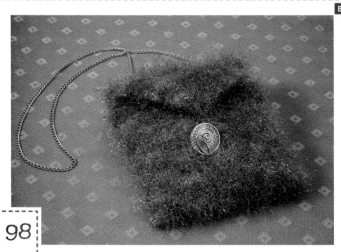

E G

F H

I

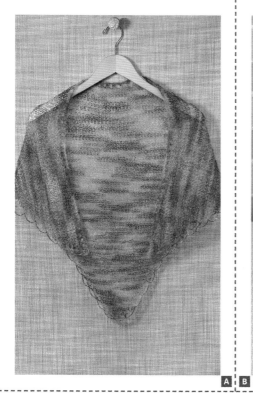

A B

C D

E

F H

G I

101

E H

F I

G

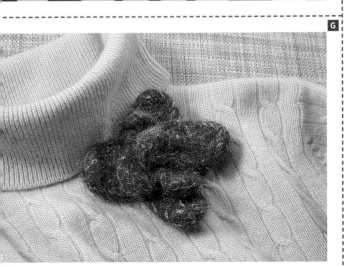

A
B
D
C

101

E

G

F H

I

101

E
H

F
I

G

A

C

101

B

D

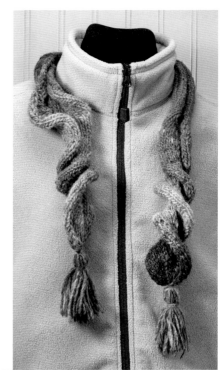

E G
F H

A

B **C**

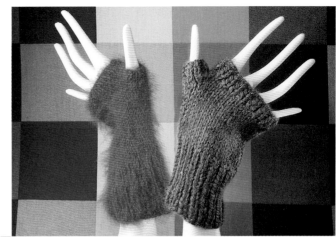

D F
E G

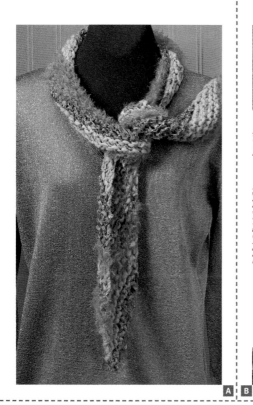

A
B

C

D F

E G

113

D F
E G

A

C

B

101

D

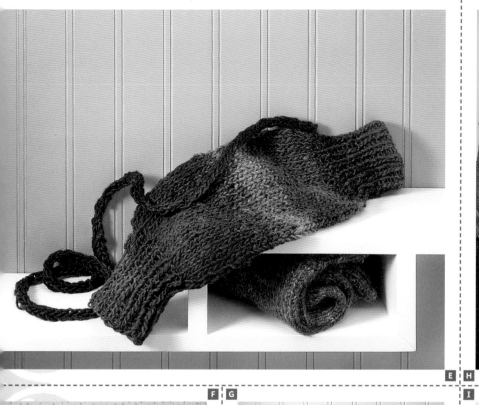

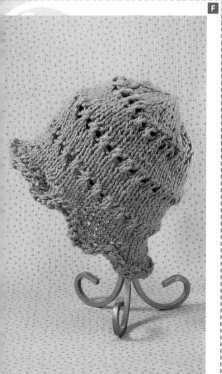

A **C**

B **D**

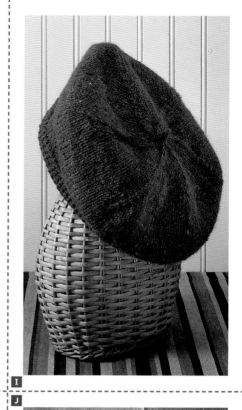

E G
F H
I
J

Beaded Diamond Bag.........

To market, to market. This open-top bag is perfect for toting home a few items. If you've never incorporated beads into your knitting, you'll find it's easy—and fun! (For advice, see sidebar on page 122.)

MEASUREMENTS	11" (28 cm) wide and 10 (12)" (25 [30.5] cm) tall
YARN	Peace Fleece, 70% wool/30% mohair, 4 oz (113 g)/200 yds (183 m), Grass Roots or Sheplova Mushroom
NEEDLES	One US 7 (4.5 mm) circular needle 16" (40 cm) long and set of US 7 (4.5 mm) double-point needles or size you need to obtain correct gauge
GAUGE	18 stitches = 4" (10 cm) in stockinette stitch
OTHER SUPPLIES	Tapestry needle, eight (for shorter bag) or twenty-four (for taller bag) ½" (1.3 cm) wooden beads

Knitting the Border

With circular needle, cast on 96 stitches. Place marker and join into a round, being careful not to twist stitches.

For shorter bag:

Work garter stitch (purl 1 round, knit 1 round) for 6 rounds.

For taller bag:

Work garter stitch (purl 1 round, knit 1 round) for 12 rounds.

Work K1, P1 rib for 6 rounds.

For both bags:

Knit 3 rounds.

Purl 1 round.

Knit 4 rounds.

Photo, p. 99

Designed by
Diana Foster

Submitted by
Lowellmountain Wools
Lowell, VT

Knitting with Beads

For one round of beads, cut off 3.5 yards of yarn, string eight beads on yarn, and set aside.

For three rounds of beads, cut off three 3.5 yard lengths of yarn, string 8 beads on each 3.5 yard length, and set aside.

To work beads into a row, begin knitting with the pre-strung length of yarn. When instructions say "place bead," move a bead up snug against right needle and knit the next stitch as usual, making sure bead stays to front of work.

Knitting the Beaded Pattern

Work 13-round pattern as follows. For 1 round of beads, work beads in Round 7. For 3 rounds of beads, work beads in Rounds 1, 7, and 13 (see chart).

Round 1: K6, *place bead, P1, K11; repeat from * to last 5 stitches, K5.

Round 2: K5, *P1, K1, P1, K9; repeat from * to last 4 stitches, K4.

Round 3: K4, *P1, K3, P1, K7; repeat from * to last 3 stitches, K3.

Round 4: K3, *P1, K5, P1, K5; repeat from * to last 2 stitches, K2.

Round 5: K2, *P1, K7, P1, K3; repeat from * to last stitch, K1.

Round 6: K1, *P1, K9, P1, K1; repeat from * to last 11 stitches, P1, K9, P1.

Round 7: *Place bead, P1, K11; repeat from *.

Round 8: *K1, P1, K9, P1; repeat from *.

Round 9: *K2, P1, K7, P1, K1; repeat from *.

Round 10: *K3, P1, K5, P1, K2; repeat from *.

Round 11: *K4, P1, K3, P1, K3; repeat from *.

Round 12: *K5, P1, K1, P1, K4; repeat from *.

Round 13: *K6, place bead, P1, K5; repeat from *.

Knit 4 rounds.

Purl 1 round.

Knit stockinette stitch for 2", decreasing 6 stitches evenly spaced in last round. You now have 90 stitches.

Decreasing for Bottom of Bag

Work decreases as follows, changing to double-point needles when necessary, probably on Round 12.

Round 1: *K13, K2tog; repeat from *. You now have 84 stitches.

Round 2: Knit.

Round 3: *K12, K2tog; repeat from *. You now have 78 stitches.

Round 4: Knit.

Continue in this manner, knitting one less stitch between decreases on decrease rounds and knitting one round even between decrease rounds through Round 14. You now have 48 stitches.

Round 15: *K6, K2tog; repeat from *. You now have 42 stitches.

Round 16: *K5, K2tog; repeat from *. You now have 36 stitches.

Continue in this manner, decreasing on every round, until 12 stitches remain.

Round 21: *K2tog; repeat from *. You now have 6 stitches.

Cut yarn, leaving a 10" tail. Thread tail onto tapestry needle and draw through remaining 6 stitches. Pull up snug and fasten off on the inside.

Knitting the Strap

Option 1: Garter Stitch Strap

With two double-point needles, pick up 5 stitches from cast-on edge.

Knit garter stitch on 5 stitches until strap measures 35".

Option 2: I-Cord

With two double-point needles, pick up 5 stitches from cast-on edge.

*Knit to last 2 stitches, bring yarn forward, slip 2 stitches purlwise. Turn.

Repeat from * until strap measures 35".

Finishing

Bind off. Sew end of strap opposite beginning.

Weave in ends. Block lightly.

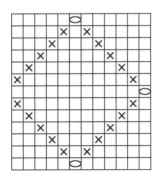

KEY

× purl

○ bead

Kirsten's Flapper Hat

This light and open cotton-and-silk cap is great when it's too warm for your winter woollies yet cool enough that you need a little something on your head.

MEASUREMENTS	Approximately 19" (48.5 cm) circumference
YARN	Misti International Misti Cotton, 83% pima cotton/17% silk, 3.5 oz (100 g)/191 yds (175 m), 387 Orchid
NEEDLES	One US 9 (5.5 mm) circular needle 16" (40 cm) long and set of US 9 (5.5 mm) double-point needles or size you need to obtain correct gauge
GAUGE	16 stitches = 4" (10 cm) in pattern
OTHER SUPPLIES	Tapestry needle
ABBREVIATIONS	inc 1 Increase 1 stitch with backward loop cast-on (see Glossary, page 228)

Knitting the Hat

With circular needle, cast on 78 stitches. Place a marker and join into a round; do not twist stitches. Change to double-point needles when necessary.

Rounds 1 and 2: Knit.

Round 3: *K3tog, inc 1, K3tog, inc 2; repeat from *. You now have 65 stitches.

Rounds 4 and 5: Knit, decreasing 1 stitch.

Round 6: *K4, K3tog, inc 1; repeat from *. You now have 54 stitches.

Rounds 7–11: Knit.

Rounds 12 and 13: *K2tog, inc 1; repeat from *.

Rounds 14–19: Knit.

Rounds 20 and 21: *K2tog, inc 1; repeat from *.

Rounds 22–27: Knit.

Photo, p. 117

Designed by
Kirsten Avent

Submitted by
Clickity Sticks & Yarns
Minneapolis, MN

Rounds 28 and 29: *K2tog, inc 1; repeat from *.

Round 30: Knit, decreasing 5 stitches evenly spaced. You now have 49 stitches.

Round 31: *K5, K2tog; repeat from *. You now have 42 stitches.

Rounds 32–33: Knit.

Round 34: *K4, K2tog; repeat from *. You now have 35 stitches.

Round 35: Knit.

Round 36: *K2tog; repeat from * to last stitch, K1. You now have 18 stitches.

Cut yarn, leaving a 10" tail. Thread tail onto tapestry needle and draw through remaining 18 stitches. Pull up snug and fasten off on the inside.

Finishing

Weave in ends.

Coffee Mitt····························

This coffee mitt will fit tight over your favorite java to go and prevent scorched hands. Practice other stitch patterns and knit up a whole series.

MEASUREMENTS	Approximately 4.5" (11.5 cm) wide at top, 3.25" (8.5 cm) wide at bottom, 4.25" (11 cm) tall
YARN	Brown Sheep Lamb's Pride, 85% wool/15% mohair, 4 oz (113 g)/ 190 yds (173.5 m), M14 Sunburst Gold (makes five mitts)
NEEDLES	US 5 (3.75 mm) straight needles or size you need to obtain correct gauge
GAUGE	20 stitches = 4" (10 cm) in pattern

Photo, p. 100

Designed by
Leanne Walker

Submitted by
KnitWit Yarn Shop
Portland, ME

Rib Pattern

Row 1: Slip 1, P3, *K2, P6; repeat from * to last 6 stitches, K2, P4.

Row 2: Slip 1, knit the knits and purl the purls.

Row 3: Repeat Row 2.

Row 4: Slip 1, P1, *K6, P2; repeat from *.

Row 5: Repeat Row 2.

Row 6: Repeat Row 2. Repeat Rows 1–6 for pattern.

Knitting the Mitt

Note: Slip stitches purlwise throughout.

Cast on 42 stitches. Work K2, P2 rib for 5 rows, slipping the first stitch of each row.

With right side facing, begin Rib Pattern. Work until 15 rows are complete.

Increase Row (wrong side): Sl 1, P1, *K1, M1, K4, M1, K1, P2; repeat from *. You now have 52 stitches.

Row 1: Slip 1, K1, *P8, K2; repeat from *.

Row 2: Slip 1, knit the knits and purl the purls (see Glossary, page 230).

Row 3: Slip 1, P4, *K2, P8; repeat from * to last 7 stitches, K2, P5.

Rows 4 and 5: Repeat Row 2.

Row 6: Sl 1, P1, *K8, P2; repeat from *.

Rows 7–11: Repeat Rows 1–5.

Bind off loosely in pattern. Cut yarn, leaving a 10" tail. Thread tail onto tapestry needle, sew back seam matching patterns. Weave in ends.

Photo, p. 98

Designed by
Elizabeth Prusiewicz

Submitted by
Knit-Knot Studio
Portland, OR

Ela's Favorite Hat

This simple hat was knitted entirely on double-point needles, and features a small rolled hem and whimsical topknots.

MEASUREMENTS Approximately 18.5" (47 cm) circumference

YARN Noro Silk Garden, 45% silk/45% kid mohair/10% lamb's wool, 1.75 oz (50 g)/109 yds (100 m), 084 Reds

NEEDLES Set of five US 8 (5 mm) double-point needles and set of five US 7 (4.5 mm) double-point needles or size you need to obtain correct gauge (or use a 16" circular and change to double points when necessary)

For Better or Worsted: Worsted-Weight Yarns

GAUGE   17 stitches = 4" (10 cm) on larger needle in stockinette stitch

OTHER SUPPLIES   Tapestry needle, stitch marker

Getting Started

With larger needles, cast on 80 stitches and divide them evenly onto four needles, 20 stitches on each needle. Place marker and join into a round, being careful not to twist stitches.

Change to smaller needle, knit 3 rounds, purl 1 round.

Repeat these 4 rounds once.

Change to larger needles and work the following sequence of rounds.

Knit 3 rounds, purl 1 round.

Knit 5 rounds, purl 1 round.

Knit 7 rounds, purl 1 round.

Knit 9 rounds, purl 1 round.

Knit 8 rounds.

Decreasing for the Crown

Round 1: *K6, K2tog; repeat from *. You now have 70 stitches.

Round 2: Knit.

Round 3: *K5, K2tog; repeat from *. You now have 60 stitches.

Round 4: Knit.

Continue in this manner, decreasing 10 stitches every other round, until 30 stitches remain.

Next Round: *K2tog; repeat from *. You now have 15 stitches.

Cut yarn, leaving a 10" tail. Thread tail onto tapestry needle, draw through remaining 15 stitches. Pull up snug and fasten off on the inside.

Finishing

If desired, make three 4-stitch I-cords (see Glossary, page 229), attach to top of hat and knot as pictured.

Weave in all ends.

Tea Cozy

Photo, p. 97

Designed by
Diana Foster

Submitted by
Lowellmountain Wools
Lowell, VT

This cozy is designed for a Rockingham Teapot from England, where they know how to make the best tea (or so their advertisement claims). Knitted in two layers, this cozy will help keep your pot warm while you knit more cozies for your friends!

MEASUREMENTS	To fit a six-cup Rockingham Teapot, 8" (20.5 cm) tall and 10" (25.5 cm) around
YARN	Peace Fleece, 70% wool/30% mohair, 4 oz (113 g)/200 yds (183 m), Ukrainian Red
NEEDLES	One US 6 (4 mm) circular needle 16" (40 cm) long and set of US 6 (4 mm) double-point needles or size you need to obtain correct gauge
GAUGE	18 stitches = 4" (10 cm) in stockinette stitch
OTHER SUPPLIES	Tapestry needle, yarn holders, marker, crochet hook size G/6 (4.5 mm)
ABBREVIATION	K1tbl Knit 1 stitch through the back loop

Knitting the Ribbing

With circular needle, cast on 88 stitches. Place marker and join into a round, being careful not to twist the stitches. Work K1tbl, P1 rib until piece measures 1" from beginning.

Knitting the Front

Divide the stitches in half, working back and forth on the first 44 stitches for the front and placing remaining 44 stitches on a holder for the back.

Row 1: Knit.

Row 2: Purl.

Row 3: Purl.

Row 4: Knit.

Repeat Rows 1–4.

Continue working back and forth on front 44 stitches as follows.

For Better or Worsted: Worsted-Weight Yarns

Rows 1 and 2: *K2, P2; repeat from *.

Rows 3 and 4: *P2, K2; repeat from *.

Repeat Rows 1–4 until piece measures 4.5" from beginning.

Place 44 front stitches on holder.

Knitting the Back

Place 44 back stitches on needle, and work as for front.

Knitting the Top

Place 44 front stitches on needle with 44 back stitches. Place marker for beginning of round and join.

Knit 2 rounds.

Purl 2 rounds.

Knit 1 round, decreasing 4 stitches evenly spaced. You now have 84 stitches.

Knit 1 round even.

Begin regular decreases for the top as follows.

Decrease Round 1: *K12, K2tog; repeat from *. You now have 78 stitches.

Decrease Round 2: Knit.

Decrease Round 3: *K11, K2tog, repeat from *. You now have 72 stitches.

Decrease Round 4: Knit.

Continue in this manner, decreasing 6 stitches on every other round, until 42 stitches remain, ending with a plain knit round.

Change to double-point needles and work decrease round only (no plain knit round between decrease rounds) until 12 stitches remain.

Next Round: *K2tog; repeat from *. You now have 6 stitches.

Next Round: *K2tog; repeat from *. You now have 3 stitches.

Knitting the Topknot

With 3 remaining stitches, knit 3-stitch I-cord (see Glossary, page 229) for 3.5". Cut yarn, fasten off, weave in end.

Tie knot in I-cord as pictured on page 97.

Knitting the Lining

Turn cozy inside out.

With circular needle, pick up and knit 44 front stitches, picking up the purl row above the ribbing on the inside.

Work back and forth in stockinette stitch (knit on right side, purl on wrong side) for 3.5", ending with a purl row. Place 44 stitches on holder.

Repeat on 44 back stitches.

Place 44 front stitches on needle with 44 back stitches. Place marker for beginning of round and join.

Knit 1 round, decreasing 4 stitches evenly spaced. You now have 84 stitches.

Knit 1 round even.

Work regular decreases as for outside until 3 stitches remain. Cut yarn, leaving an 8" tail. Thread tail on tapestry needle and draw through the remaining 3 stitches. Pull up snug, fasten off, and weave in end.

Finishing

With crochet hook and two layers held together, make 30 single crochets around spout and handle openings, beginning at ribbing and ending with slip stitch in first single crochet.

Weave in ends.

Little Ruff

This fanciful ruff can be worn with a little black dress or with a T-shirt and jeans. It is shaped with a series of short rows on both sides of a central spine, and you can make it as wide or as long as your amount of yarn allows.

Photo, p. 109

MEASUREMENTS	Approximately 4" (10 cm) wide and 16" (40.5 cm) long with a 1" (2.5 cm) center front overlap
YARN	Noro Cash Iroha, 40% silk/30% lamb's wool/20% cashmere/10% nylon, 1.5 oz (43 g)/99 yds (91 m), 22 Red
NEEDLES	US 7 (4.5 mm) straight needles or size you need to obtain correct gauge
GAUGE	18 stitches = 4" (10 cm) in garter stitch
OTHER SUPPLIES	One ¾" (2 cm) button

Knitting the Ruff

Cast on 18 stitches. See Glossary, page 234, for short row instructions and explanation of WT.

Row 1: K2, WT.

Row 2: K2.

Row 3: K4, WT.

Row 4: K4.

Row 5: K6, WT.

Row 6: K6.

Row 7: K18.

You are now at the other side of the ruff.

Repeat Rows 1–7 until spine measures 15", ending with Row 6.

Buttonhole Row: K8, K2tog, yo, K8.

Repeat Rows 1–7 until spine measures 16". Bind off.

Finishing

Weave in ends, sew button about 1" from end of ruff without the buttonhole. Wash the ruff, lay the spine out flat, fluff up the ruffles, and allow to dry.

Designed by
Judith Durant
Lowell, MA

Ribbed Cap

This hat was born as my husband mourned the loss of his favorite ribbed hat, which he had purchased in London a few years ago. As the original hat was knit on what I estimated to be a size 0 needle, I politely told him he could forget about receiving a handmade replica any time soon. We did arrive at this accepted alternative, knit in worsted weight on a size 7 needle.

Photo, p. 100

Designed by
Hannah Fettig

Submitted by
KnitWit Yarn Shop
Portland, ME

MEASUREMENTS	One size fits all
YARN	Hat A: Cascade 220, 100% Peruvian highland merino wool, 3.5 oz (100 g)/220 yards (201 m), Color 2427
	Hat B: The Fibre Company Fauna, 70% alpaca/30% merino, 1.75 oz (50 g)/100 yards (91 m), Fawn
NEEDLES	One US 7 (4.5 mm) circular needle 16" (40 cm) long and set of US 7 (4.5 mm) double-point needles or size you need to obtain correct gauge
GAUGE	20 stitches = 4" (10 cm) in pattern
OTHER SUPPLIES	Tapestry needle

Getting Started

Cast on 96 stitches. Join into a round, being careful not to twist stitches.

Work K2, P2 rib until piece measures 6.5", or desired length.

Decreasing for the Top

Decrease Round 1: *K2tog, P2tog; repeat from *. You now have 48 stitches.

Work K1, P1 rib for 3 rounds.

Next Decrease Round: *K2tog; repeat from *. You now have 24 stitches.

Next Decrease Round: *K2tog; repeat from *. You now have 12 stitches.

Finishing

Break yarn, leaving a 12" tail. Thread tail into tapestry needle and draw through remaining stitches. Pull up snug and fasten off on the inside. Weave in end.

Bamboo Baby··············

T he asymmetrical closing on this baby sweater sets it apart from the ordinary. The eyelets in the trim double as buttonholes, and you can use more or fewer buttons than shown here—simply line them up with the eyelets.

Designed by
Tamara Del Sonno

Submitted by
Clickity Sticks & Yarns
Minneapolis, MN

Photo, p. 113

MEASUREMENTS	To fit a newborn, 17" (43 cm) chest
YARN	South West Trading Company Bamboo, 100% bamboo, 3.5 oz (100 g)/250 yds (229 m), Bougainville
NEEDLES	US 6 (4 mm) straight needles or size you need to obtain correct gauge
GAUGE	18 stitches = 4" (10 cm) in stockinette stitch
OTHER SUPPLIES	5 × ⅞" (2.2 cm) buttons, sewing needle and thread, tapestry needle

Knitting the Fronts (Make 2)

Cast on 5 stitches.

Row 1: K2, yo, knit to end of row.

Row 2: K1, Kfb, knit to end of row.

Repeat Rows 1 and 2 until piece measures 4". Place sleeve markers. Continue in garter stitch until there are 50 stitches. Place shoulder markers.

Knitting the Front Shoulder

Row 3: K2, yo, knit to end of row.

Row 4: K1, K2tog, knit to end of row.

Repeat Rows 3 and 4 eight times.

Row 5: K2, *K2tog, yo; repeat from * to last 2 stitches, knit to end of row.

Rows 6–8: Knit.

Bind off.

Knitting the Back

Cast on 38 stitches. Knit 3 rows.

Next row: K2, *yo, K2tog; repeat from *.

Continue in garter stitch (knit every row) until piece measures 4". Place sleeve markers on each end. Continue until piece measures 6.5". Bind off all stitches.

Sewing the Shoulder Seams

Place right sides together and sew from shoulder marker to bind-off edge of fronts to back section.

Knitting the Sleeves

Pick up and knit 24 stitches evenly between the marked rows on the front and back. Knit even for 3.5". Bind off.

Finishing

Sew side and underarm seams. Weave in all ends. Attach buttons along front opening and at right side seam. Block.

Photo, p. 120

Designed by
Sue Dial
Harvest Moon Handspun

Submitted by
Baskets of Yarn
Charlotte, NC

Easy Mittens

These handspun, hand-painted mittens are absolutely one of a kind, and are the perfect rationalization for going ahead and splurging on some one-of-a-kind yarn. The pattern is sized for both small and large adult hands, so why not knit a pair for a friend, too?

MEASUREMENTS Adult small (large) 9.5" (24 cm) from cuff to tip, 7 (8)" (18 [20.5] cm) around

YARN Harvest Moon Handspun Handpainted Bulky Singles, lamb's wool/mohair/German angora, 2.4 oz (68 g)/120 yds (110 m), 8 wpi

NEEDLES	Set of US 6 (4 mm) double-point needles or size you need to obtain correct gauge
GAUGE	20 stitches and 28 rows = 4" (10 cm) in stockinette stitch
OTHER SUPPLIES	Tapestry needle, markers
ABBREVIATIONS	pm Place marker sm Slip marker M1 Make 1 increase (see Glossary, page 231)

Knitting the Cuff

Cast on 32 (36) stitches with the backward loop method (see Glossary, page 228). Divide stitches evenly among three needles as follows

Needle 1	12 stitches
Needle 2	10 (12) stitches
Needle 3	10 (12) stitches

Join into a round, being careful not to twist stitches.

Knit 22 (26) rounds (approximately 3.5") to thumb gusset.

Next Round: *K8 (9), M1; repeat from *. You now have 36 (40) stitches.

Knitting the Thumb Gusset

Round 1: K2, pm, M1, K1, M1, pm, knit to end of round.

Round 2: Knit.

Round 3: Knit to marker, sm, M1, knit to next marker, M1, sm, knit to end of round.

Repeat Rounds 2 and 3 until there are 11 (13) stitches between the markers. Place these 11 (13) stitches on holder.

Knitting the Hand

Work stockinette stitch (knit every round) on remaining 35 (39) stitches until mitten reaches top of pinky (approximately 4" from end of gusset).

Decreasing for Top of Hand

For size small:

*K5, K2tog; repeat from *. You now have 30 stitches.

For size large:

*K11, K2tog; repeat from *. You now have 36 stitches.

Knit 2 rounds.

*K4, K2tog; repeat from *. You now have 30 stitches.

For both sizes:

Knit 2 rounds.

*K3, K2tog; repeat from *. You now have 24 stitches.

Knit 2 rounds.

*K2, K2tog; repeat from *. You now have 18 stitches.

Knit 1 round.

*K2tog; repeat from *. You now have 9 stitches.

Break yarn, leaving a 10" tail. Thread tail onto tapestry needle, draw through remaining 9 stitches. Pull snug and fasten off on the inside.

Knitting the Thumb

Place 11 (13) thumb stitches from holder onto needles as follows:

Needle 1	4 (5) stitches
Needle 2	4 (5) stitches
Needle 3	3 stitches

Pick up 3 stitches from hand to close the gap. You now have 14 (16) stitches.

Knit 14 rounds.

*K2tog; repeat from *. You now have 7 (8) stitches.

Cut yarn, leaving a 10" tail. Thread tail onto tapestry needle, draw through remaining 7 (8) stitches. Pull up snug and fasten off on the inside. Work second mitten.

Finishing

Weave in ends. Block if desired.

Be-Ribboned Booties·······

Photo, p. 105

Pair these with the Be-Ribboned Bonnet on page 76 for a simple but special baby gift. Garter stitch allows for baby's rapid growth, and the booties are shaped to stay on small feet! (Read about the environmentally friendly yarn on the bonnet page.)

Designed by
Diana Lischer Goodband

Submitted by
Green Mountain Spinnery
Putney, VT

MEASUREMENTS	3" (7.5 cm) cuff and 4.5" (11.5 cm) foot
YARN	Green Mountain Spinnery, 50% wool/50% alpaca, 2 oz (57 g)/180 yds (165 m), Natural
NEEDLES	US 4 (3.5 mm) straight needles or size you need to obtain correct gauge
GAUGE	22 stitches = 4" (10 cm) in stockinette stitch
OTHER SUPPLIES	1 yd (1 m) of ¼" (6 mm) ribbon for ties, scrap yarn or stitch holders, tapestry needle

Knitting the Leg

Cast on 38 stitches. Work in garter stitch (knit every row) until there are 14 ridges on both sides of work. (This will be 27 or 28 rows, depending on cast-on method.)

Eyelet Row: K1, *K2tog, yo; repeat from * to last stitch, K1.

Knit 5 rows, decreasing 3 stitches evenly spaced on fifth row. You now have 35 stitches.

Dividing for the Heel

Knit 24 and place last 11 stitches on holder.

Turn and knit 13, place last 11 stitches on another holder.

Continue back and forth on center 13 stitches for 20 rows (10 garter ridges). This forms the top of the bootie. Break yarn.

Forming the Heel

Place 11 stitches from right holder onto needle, attach yarn, and pick up and knit 11 stitches from right edge of bootie top; knit 13 top-of-foot stitches; pick up and knit 11 stitches from left edge of bootie top; knit 11 stitches from holder. You now have 57 stitches.

Knit 9 rows.

Shaping the Foot

Row 1: K1, K2tog, K22, K2tog, K3, K2tog, K22, K2tog, K1.

Row 2: Knit.

Row 3: K1, K2tog, K20, K2tog, K3, K2tog, K20, K2tog, K1.

Row 4: Knit.

Row 5: K1, K2tog, K18, K2tog, K3, K2tog, K18, K2tog, K1.

Bind off loosely. Cut yarn, leaving a 10" tail.

Finishing

Thread yarn onto tapestry needle and sew together bottom of foot and back of bootie, catching only the outside of each stitch for a flat seam. Weave in ends.

Wash in warm water with a vegetable-based soap. Roll in a towel, press out excess moisture, lay flat to dry.

Cut ribbon in half and thread half through the eyelets of each bootie.

Twirly-Top Toque

This lacy, flat-topped cap is cute and fun to knit. It begins at the bottom with a simple lace pattern and then swirls at the top for a smart finish. You could also skip the top part and wear this as a headband.

*Photo,
p. 110*

MEASUREMENTS	Approximately 20" (51 cm) circumference
YARN	Misti Alpaca, 100% alpaca, 1.75 oz (50 g)/109 yds (100 m), 6309 Ocean Mist Teal
NEEDLES	One size US 7 (4.5 mm) circular needle 16" (40 cm) long and set of US 7 (4.5 mm) double-point needles or size you need to obtain correct gauge
GAUGE	16 stitches = 4" (10 cm) in pattern
OTHER SUPPLIES	Stitch marker, tapestry needle

Knitting the Band

With circular needle, cast on 84 stitches. Place marker and join into a round, being careful not to twist the stitches.

Purl 4 rounds.

Knit 1 round.

Begin Lace Pattern Stitch (see at right) and work until piece measures 5" from cast-on edge.

Purl 5 rounds.

Knit 1 round.

For headband, bind off here.

Knitting the Twirly Top

Decrease for the flat top as follows, changing to double-point needles when necessary.

Round 1: *K2tog, yo, K8, K3tog, yo, K8; repeat from *. You now have 80 stitches.

Round 2 and all even-numbered rounds through 16: Knit.

Round 3: *K3tog, yo, K7; repeat from *. You now have 72 stitches.

Round 5: *K3tog, yo, K6; repeat from *. You now have 64 stitches.

Round 7: *K3tog, yo, K5; repeat from *. You now have 56 stitches.

Round 9: *K3tog, yo, K4; repeat from *. You now have 48 stitches.

Designed by
Tamara Del Sonno

Submitted by
Clickity Sticks & Yarns
Minneapolis, MN

Lace Pattern Stitch

Round 1: *K1, yo, ssk, K2, K2tog, yo; repeat from *,

Round 2: Knit.

Round 3: *K2, yo, ssk, K2tog, yo, K1; repeat from *.

Round 4: Knit.
Repeat Rounds 1–4 for pattern.

Round 11: *K3tog, yo, K3; repeat from *. You now have 40 stitches.

Round 13: *K3tog, yo, K2; repeat from *. You now have 32 stitches.

Round 15: *K3tog, yo, K1; repeat from *. You now have 24 stitches.

Round 17: *K3tog, yo; repeat from *. You now have 16 stitches.

Break yarn, leaving a 10" tail. Thread tail onto tapestry needle and draw through remaining stitches. Snug up, fasten off on inside, weave in end.

Finishing

With wrong side facing, loosely whipstitch the first and fifth purl rounds together at top to help hold the ridge.

Weave in ends.

Hiker Socks

What's so great about these socks? The Broken Garter Pattern Stitch makes them thick and comfy to cushion hardworking feet. The pattern does incredible things for hand-painted yarns: only one strand of yarn—no complicated color changes. An added bonus—they stretch amazingly to fit growing feet, so they're great for kids!

Photo, p. 120

Designed by
Margaret K. Radcliffe

Submitted by
Maggie's Rags
Blacksburg, VA

MEASUREMENTS **Small:** 5.75–7.5" (14.5–19 cm) foot length, 6.5–8" (16.5–20.5) foot circumference

Medium: 7.75–9.5" (19.5–24 cm) foot length, 7–9" (18–23 cm) foot circumference

Large: 9.5–11.25" (19.5–28.5 cm) foot length, 8.5–10.5" (21.5–26.5 cm) foot circumference

NOTE The instructions for the different sizes appear as small (medium, large).

YARN   Tess Designer Yarns Superwash Merino, 100% wool, 8 oz (228 g)/ 560 yds (512 m), Confetti

NEEDLES   Set of US 4 (3.5 mm) double-point needles or size you need to obtain correct gauge

GAUGE   22 stitches = 4" in pattern

Knitting the Leg

Cast on 33 (39, 45) stitches.

Arrange stitches onto three double-point needles as follows:

Needle 1 15 (18, 21) stitches

Needle 2 9 (12, 12) stitches

Needle 3 9 (9, 12) stitches

Join into a round, being careful not to twist stitches.

Work in Broken Garter Pattern Stitch (see at right) until piece measures 5 (6, 7)" from beginning.

Knitting the Heel Flap

Slip all stitches from Needle 3 onto Needle 2. You now have stitches on two needles as follows:

Needle 1 15 (18, 21) stitches

Needle 2 18 (21, 24) stitches

Turn and work back and forth on stitches on Needle 2 only.

Row 1 (wrong side):

For size small and large: *P3, K3; repeat from *.

For size medium: *P3, K3; repeat to last 3 stitches, P3.

Row 2 (right side):

For size small and large: *K3, P3; repeat from *.

For size medium: P3, *K3, P3; repeat from *.

Repeat Rows 1 and 2 until 19 (23, 27) rows have been completed.

Broken Garter Pattern Stitch

Round 1: *K3, P3; repeat from * to last 3 stitches, K3.

Round 2: *P3, K3; repeat from * to last 3 stitches, P3.

Repeat Rounds 1 and 2 for pattern.

For Better or Worsted: Worsted-Weight Yarns

Shaping the Heel

Row 1 (right side): K11 (13, 14), K2tog, K1, turn.

Row 2 (wrong side): Slip 1, K5 (6, 5), K2tog, K1, turn.

Row 3: Slip 1, knit to 1 stitch before the gap formed by last turn, K2tog, K1, turn.

Repeat Row 3 on both right- and wrong-side rows until all heel stitches have been worked.

Note: On the last 2 rows, you may not have enough stitches to work the last K1. If this happens, simply ignore the K1, turn, and work the next row.

You now have 12 (13, 14) heel stitches. This is the Bottom Needle. The stitches you have not been working are on the Top Needle.

Break yarn. Using an empty needle, attach yarn and work across Top Needle in Broken Garter pattern as established.

Using an empty needle, now called the First Side Needle, pick up and knit 11 (13, 15) stitches along edge of heel flap. With same needle, knit about half the stitches from Bottom Needle.

Using an empty needle, now called Second Side Needle, knit the remaining stitches from Bottom Needle and with the same needle pick up and knit 11 (13, 15) stitches along the other edge of the heel flap.

Mark this point as the beginning of the round. You now have 49 (57, 65) stitches on three needles as follows:

Top Needle 15 (18, 21) stitches

Both Side Needles 34 (39, 44) stitches

Knitting the Gussets

Round 1:

Top Needle	Work Broken Garter pattern as established.
First Side Needle	Purl.
Second Side Needle	Purl.

Round 2:

Top Needle	Work Broken Garter pattern as established.
First Side Needle	K2tog, knit to end.
Second Side Needle	Knit to last 2 stitches, K2tog.

Repeat Rounds 1 and 2 until 33 (39, 45) stitches remain.

Leave stitches on Top Needle as they are and redistribute stitches between side needles so you have stitches on three needles as follows:

Top Needle	15 (18, 21) stitches
First Side Needle	9 (12, 12) stitches
Second Side Needle	9 (9, 12) stitches

Knitting the Foot

Continue in Broken Garter pattern on all stitches until foot measures 1 (1.5, 1.75)" less than desired finished length. End your last round after completing stitches on First Side Needle.

Shaping the Toe

Needle 1	Knit to last 3 stitches, K2tog, K1.
Needle 2	Knit.
Needle 3	K1, ssk, K4 (6, 7), K2tog. You may need to knit a few stitches from Needle 1 to Needle 3; or you may have a few stitches left on Needle 3—slip them to Needle 1.

You now have 30 (36, 42) stitches total arranged with half on Needle 2 and the other half divided evenly between Needle 1 and Needle 3.

Decrease Round:

Needle 1	Knit to last 3 stitches, K2tog, K1.
Needle 2	K1, ssk, knit to last 3 stitches, K2tog, K1.
Needle 3	K1, ssk, knit to end of needle.

Knit 1 round.

Repeat these 2 rounds for a total of 3 (4, 5) times. You now have 18 (20, 22) stitches.

Work Decrease Round two times. You now have 10 (12, 14) stitches.

Knit the stitches from Needle 1 onto Needle 3. Your stitches are now evenly divided onto two needles.

Finishing

Cut the yarn leaving, a 12" tail, and graft toe stitches together with Kitchener Stitch (see Glossary, page 230). Weave in ends.

Sofia Cowl

A lace cowl is a cozy and feminine alternative to a scarf—but don't let the lace part scare you off. This cowl uses a very straightforward pattern—there are only two rows to it, and one of them is plain knit!

MEASUREMENTS	8" (20.5 cm) tall and 22"(56 cm) around
YARN	Karabella Boise, 50% cashmere/50% wool, 1.75 oz (50 g)/164 yds (150 m)
NEEDLES	One US 6 (4 mm) circular needle 20" (51 cm) long or size you need to obtain correct gauge
GAUGE	19 stitches = 4" (10 cm) in pattern, 22 stitches = 4" (10 cm) in stockinette stitch
OTHER SUPPLIES	Stitch marker, tapestry needle
ABBREVIATION	Sl 1, K2tog, psso Slip 1 Knit the next 2 stitches together, pass the slipped stitch over the 2 knitted-together stitches and off the needle

Photo, p. 113

Designed by
Jessie Dotson

Submitted by
Stash—Yarn + Inspiration
Berkeley, CA

For Better or Worsted: Worsted-Weight Yarns

Pattern Notes

The beginning of round marker will not stay directly above the start of your piece; the Lace Pattern Stitch (see at right) works up on a bias and the marker will move with that slant.

Be careful not to let the marker slide under the last yarnover of the lace pattern. The yarnover should always be before the stitch marker.

Slip all stitches knitwise.

Knitting the Cowl

Cast on 108 stitches. Place marker and join into a round, being careful not to twist stitches.

Work lace pattern until piece measures 8" from cast-on edge.

Bind off loosely with suspended bind-off (see Glossary, page 234).

Finishing

Weave in ends. Block if desired.

One-Skein Felted·············· Purse with One-Skein Flower

The bag pictured is actually two one-skein projects—the bag and the optional flower. Knit the bag and use it without the flower. Knit the flower and use it on something other than the bag. Either way, it's double the fun!

Lace Pattern Stitch

Round 1: Knit.

Round 2: *Sl 1, K2tog, psso, yo, K1, yo; repeat from *.
Repeat Rounds 1 and 2 for pattern.

Photo, p. 99

Designed by
Flo Burdick

Submitted by
Enticements
Decatur, IL

For Better or Worsted: Worsted-Weight Yarns

One-Skein Felted Purse

MEASUREMENTS **Bag:** Approximately 9" (23 cm) wide and 4" (10 cm) tall with 4" (10 cm) base, felted (*Note:* Exact finished measurements will be determined by the yarn and the point at which you stop felting.)

YARN Brown Sheep Nature Spun, 100% wool, 3.5 oz (100 g)/245 yds (224 m), N108 Cherry Delight (*Note:* Yarn is used doubled throughout.)

NEEDLES One US 10.5 (6.5 mm) circular needle 24" (60 cm) long or size you need to obtain correct gauge

GAUGE Approximately 10 stitches = 4" (10 cm) in stockinette stitch, prefelted

OTHER SUPPLIES Magnetic closure, stitch markers, tapestry needle, coilless pin for flower

Knitting the Base

With two strands of wool, cast on 20 stitches. Knit back and forth 30 rows and place marker.

Continuing with same working yarn, pick up and knit 15 stitches along side of base. Place second marker.

Pick up and knit 20 stitches along cast-on row. Place third marker.

Pick up and knit 15 stitches along other side. Place fourth marker. Use a different-color marker here to indicate beginning of round.

Knitting the Sides

Join into a round and knit 4 rounds.

Decreases are worked only on the short side of the purse as follows.

Decrease Round 1: K20; slip marker, K2tog, K11, K2tog, slip marker; K20; slip marker, K2tog, K11, K2tog, slip marker. You now have 13 stitches on short sides.

Knit 4 rounds.

Decrease Round 2: K20; slip marker, K2tog, K9, K2tog, slip marker; K20; slip marker, K2tog, K9, K2tog, slip marker. You now have 11 stitches on short sides.

Knit 4 rounds.

Continue in this manner, decreasing 2 stitches between the markers on the short sides and knitting 4 rounds even between the decrease rounds until you have 7 stitches on short sides.

Last Decrease Round: K20; slip marker, (k2tog) three times, K1, slip marker; K20; slip marker, (K2tog) three times, K1, slip marker. You now have 4 stitches on short sides.

Knit 4 rounds.

Bind off until you have 3 stitches remaining on left needle. Transfer 1 stitch from right needle to left.

Knitting the Handle

Work these 4 stitches back and forth in garter stitch (knit 1 row, purl 1 row) until strap is 14" long. Bind off.

Twist the strap a few times and sew it to the opposite side of the bag.

Knitting the Clasp Reinforcements

With two strands of yarn, cast on 10 stitches.

Knit 10 rows.

Bind off. Felt with the bag as described below.

Felting the Bag

Set the washer for the lowest water level, longest washing cycle, and hottest temperature. Drizzle in Eucalan soap as the washer fills with hot water. Place purse and reinforcement piece in a net bag. Start the machine and check the items after one wash cycle. If you can still see the stitches, set the wash cycle to begin again. Repeat the cycle until stitches are no longer visible in the pieces. Eucalan soap does not need rinsing, so proceed to a spin cycle for a minute or so. Stuff the purse with plastic grocery bags and allow to dry.

Finishing

Cut the reinforcement swatch in half.

Poke the prongs of the clasp through the wool reinforcement pieces.

Slip on clasp backs and bend prongs to secure.

Sew the clasp reinforcement to the inside of the purse near the center.

One-Skein Flower

MEASUREMENTS	Approximately 6" (15 cm) in diameter (*Note:* Exact finished measurements will be determined by the yarn and the point at which you stop felting.)
YARN	Anny Blatt Albatros, 43% wool/57% polymid, 1.75 oz (50 g)/ 49 yds (45 m), 749 Beryl
NEEDLE	One US 15 (10 cm) circular needle 16" (40 cm) long
GAUGE	8 stitches = 4" (10 cm) in stockinette stitch

Knitting the Flower

Cast on 55 stitches.

Row 1: *K1, P1; repeat from *.

Row 2: *P1, K1; repeat from *.

Row 3: K1, *K1, Kfb, K1; repeat from *.

Row 4: *P1, K2; repeat from *.

Row 5: *K3, Kfb; repeat from *.

Row 6: *P1, K3; repeat from *.

Binding Off for Ruffle

Bind off 1 stitch.

Cast on 2 stitches and transfer to left needle. Bind off 3 stitches.

Repeat this pattern of casting on 2 and binding off 3 until all stitches are bound off.

Finishing

Roll curly strip into flower and stitch together at several points to hold the shape. Sew flower to purse or attach a pin back, and wear it everywhere!

Felted Evening Bag with
Ribbon Embroidery . . . .

Photo, p. 108

The ribbon embroidery on this bag elevates it to "evening wear" status. You may also embellish with rhinestones, crystals, or whatever you like. This bag is fully lined and closes with a magnetic snap.

MEASUREMENTS	Approximately 9" (23 cm) wide and 6" (15 cm) tall with a 29" (73.5 cm) handle (*Note:* Exact finished measurements will be determined by the yarn and the point at which you stop felting.)
YARN	Cascade 220, 100% wool, 3.5 oz (100 g)/220 yds (201 m), Color 8901
NEEDLES	One US 10 or 10.5 (6 or 6.5 mm) circular needle 24" (40 cm) long and set of double-point needles same size or size you need to obtain correct gauge
GAUGE	Approximately 12–14 stitches = 4" (10 cm) before felting
OTHER SUPPLIES	One US G/6 (4.5 mm) or H/8 (5 mm) crochet hook; embroidery ribbon: 4 mm green and purple, 7 mm white; beads: a few bugle and seed beads; ½ yd (46 cm) lining fabric; magnetic closure; number 18 or 20 chenille needle; matching sewing thread

Designed by
Jane M. Brown

Submitted by
Craftique/Never Enough Knitting Wheaton, IL

Knitting the Bag

With circular needle, cast on 80 stitches and join into a round, being careful not to twist stitches.

Knit every round until piece measures 8" from beginning.

Beginning 2 stitches before the first cast-on stitch, bind off 44 stitches. You now have 36 stitches.

Work stockinette stitch back and forth for 8 rows.

Next Row: Decrease 1 stitch at the beginning and end of the row. You now have 42 stitches.

Next Row: Purl.

Repeat these 2 rows until 10 stitches remain.

Bind off while decreasing each end.

Crocheting the Edge

Single crochet along edge of bag.

Cut yarn and fasten off.

Knitting the Handle

Using two double-point needles, cast on 5 stitches.

Work 5-stitch I-cord (see Glossary, page 229) for 46" (or 24" for short handle.) Stitch handle to sides of bag.

Felting the Bag

Set the machine for the lowest water level, longest washing cycle, and hottest temperature. Place the bag in the washing machine and check felting progress at 5-minute intervals until desired shrinkage is achieved. Don't shrink too tight or it will be difficult to embroider.

Embroidering

Following illustration below, sew ribbon and beads to flap with needle and thread.

Finishing

Line with fabric if desired. Attach magnetic snap.

embroidery pattern

Basic Tam with Flowers·······

Seed Stitch gives this simple tam loads of texture. It is guaranteed to keep you warm. Add the optional flowers for extra good looks.

MEASUREMENTS	Approximately 19" (48.5 cm) circumference, unstretched
YARN	Cottage Craft Woollens 2-Ply, 100% wool, 4 oz (113 g)/272 yds (248 m)
NEEDLES	Set of US 6 (4 mm) double-point needles or size you need to obtain correct gauge
GAUGE	21 stitches = 4" (10 cm) in pattern
OTHER SUPPLIES	Tapestry needle
ABBREVIATION	Pfb Purl into front and back of stitch

Knitting the Band

Cast on 90 stitches and place 30 stitches on each of three needles. Join into a round, being careful not to twist stitches.

Place a marker for beginning of round and work K1, P1 rib until piece measures approx 1¾" from beginning.

Increase Round: *K1, P1, K1, Pfb; repeat from * 20 more times, work even in established rib to end of round. You now have 111 stitches.

Knitting the Body

Begin Seed Stitch (see at right) and work until piece measures approx 3½" from ribbing.

Next Round: Purl, increasing 1 stitch at end of round. You now have 112 stitches.

Knit 1 round.

Purl 1 round.

Photo, p.116

Designed by
Kathy Lingusky

Submitted by
South Pine Ranch
Conifer, CO

Seed Stitch

(worked in the round on add odd number of stitches)

Round 1: *K1, P1; repeat from *.

Round 2: *P1, K1; repeat from *.

Decreasing for the Crown

Round 1: *K12, K2tog; repeat from *. You now have 104 stitches.

Round 2: Knit.

Round 3: *K11, K2tog; repeat from *. You now have 96 stitches.

Round 4: Knit.

Continue in this manner, working 1 fewer stitch between decreases and knitting one row even between decrease rounds, until 8 stitches remain. Cut the yarn, leaving a 12" tail. Thread tail onto tapestry needle, draw tail through remaining stitches, pull up snug to close top of tam, and fasten off. Weave in end.

Optional Flowers

For each flower you will need approx 15 yards of wool in same weight as wool used for tam. Use same-size needles used for tam.

Cast on 66 stitches.

Rows 1–4: Work stockinette stitch (knit 1 row, purl 1 row).

Row 5: *K6, twist (see Doing the Twist, at left); repeat from * to last 6 stitches, K6.

Row 6: K1, *K2tog; repeat from * to last stitch, K1. You now have 34 stitches.

Row 7: K1, *P2tog; repeat from * to last stitch, K1. You now have 18 stitches.

Row 8: K1, *K2tog; repeat from * to last stitch, K1. You now have 10 stitches.

Cut yarn, leaving a 12" tail. Thread tail onto tapestry needle, draw through remaining 10 stitches. Pull up snug to form flower and fasten off on the inside. Use remaining tail to sew flower to tam.

Doing the Twist

Hold your needles point to point, ready to knit the next stitch. Keeping the left needle stationary, rotate the right needle 360 degrees by turning the point down and away from you, then up and in front of the left needle. Resume knitting as usual.

Mel's Funky 3-Way Hat......

This hat can be worn as a headband, hat, or neck warmer. The sample shown was knitted of undyed Lamb's Pride worsted and space-dyed with Louet's Gaywool dyes in cypress, hibiscus, saltbush, and mushroom.

Photo, p. 119

Designed by
Melanie Wagner

Submitted by
Mad About Ewes
Lewisburg, PA

MEASUREMENTS	**Adult small:** 18 " (45.5 cm) around and 9" (23 cm) tall
	Adult medium: 20" (51 cm) around and 9" (23 cm) tall
	Adult large: 22" (56 cm) around and 9" (23 cm) tall
YARN	Brown Sheep Company Lamb's Pride, 85% wool/15% mohair, 4 oz (113 g)/190 yds (174 m)
NEEDLES	One each US 7 and 8 (4.5 and 5 mm) circular needles 16" (40 cm) long or size you need to obtain correct gauge; set of US 7 (4.5 mm) double-point needles
GAUGE	20 stitches = 4" (10 cm) in stockinette stitch

Knitting the Hat

With smaller circular needle, cast on 92 (100, 108) stitches. Place marker and join into a round, being careful not to twist stitches.

Work K2, P2 rib for 6 rounds.

Change to larger needle and work stockinette stitch (knit every round) until piece measures 8" from beginning.

Change to smaller needle and work K2, P2 rib for 6 rounds.

Bind off loosely in rib.

Making the Cords (make 2)

Using two double-point needles, cast on 3 stitches and work 3-stitch I-cord (see Glossary, page 229) for 12". Bind off, leaving a 10" tail.

Attaching the I-Cord

Lay hat flat on table with ribbing at top and bottom. Using the 10" tails, sew cords to lower edge of ribbing at top of hat, about 1" in from the sides.

The hat can now be worn three ways.

1. For a headband, fold down top part of hat (the part with the I-cord ties) about three-quarters of the way and use I-cord to tie a bow at the side.

2. For a hat, use I-cord to gather shut the top of the hat.

3. For a neck warmer, tie I-cord loosely and wear around neck.

·······Muff or "Smitten"

This muff can be worn by an individual or it can be used by a couple (who are *smitten* with each other) who want to hold hands within the warmth of a common mitten. If used as a muff, it can be hung around the neck with the added I-cord. The color variation in Kureyon yarn adds fun to the knitting and the wearing.

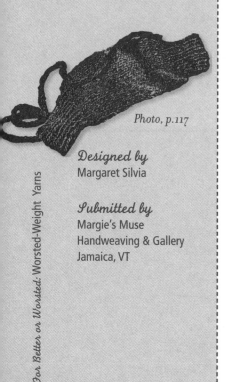

Photo, p.117

Designed by
Margaret Silvia

Submitted by
Margie's Muse
Handweaving & Gallery
Jamaica, VT

MEASUREMENTS	Approximately 16" (40.5 cm) long and 11" (28 cm) around
YARN	Noro Kureyon, 100% wool, 1.75 oz (50 g)/109 yds (100 m), color 148
NEEDLES	One set each of US 10.5 (6.5 mm) and US 11 (8 mm) double-point needles or size you need to obtain correct gauge
GAUGE	14 stitches = 4" (10 cm) in stockinette stitch
ABBREVIATIONS	M1 Make 1 increase (see Glossary, page 231)

Getting Started

With smaller needles, cast on 24 stitches and place 8 stitches on each of three needles. Join into a round, being careful not to twist stitches.

Knitting the First Cuff

Rounds 1–16: *K1, P1; repeat from * to end of round.

Knitting the Muff

Change to larger needles and knit 1 round.

Increase Round: *K2, M1; repeat from * to end of round. You now have 36 stitches.

Work stockinette stitch (knit every round) until piece measures approx 9" from end of ribbing.

Knitting the Second Cuff

Change to smaller needles.

Decrease Round: *K1, K2tog; repeat to end of round. You now have 24 stitches.

Rounds 1–16: *K1, P1; repeat from * to end of round.

Bind off in rib.

Making the I cord

Leaving a tail for attaching to muff, with larger dpn, work a 3-stitch I-cord (see Glossary, page 229) until it measures 52" or desired length. Bind off, leaving a tail for attaching to muff.

Finishing

Sew or tie ends of I-cord to muff where the cuff meets the body on each end. Weave in ends.

Photo, p.117

Designed by
Marji B. LaFreniere

Submitted by
Marji's Yarncrafts
Granby, CT

Super Simple Triangle Shawl

This is an infinitely wearable shawl. Finished with an optional reverse single crochet edge, the shawl is light and clings nicely to the shoulders. It is stretchy enough to tie in front and wear all day and soft enough to scrunch up around your neck inside your coat.

MEASUREMENTS	Approximately 59" (150 cm) wide and 22" (56 cm) deep
YARN	Mountain Colors Wool Crepe, 100% wool, 12 oz (340 g)/1450 yds (1326 m), Rosehip
NEEDLE	One US 8 (5 mm) circular needle 29" (74 cm) long or size you need to obtain correct gauge
GAUGE	18 stitches = 4" (10 cm) in garter stitch
OTHER SUPPLIES	One size G/6 (4.5 mm) or H/8 (5 mm) crochet hook (optional)
ABBREVIATIONS	M1 Make 1 increase (see Glossary, page 231)
NOTE	The instructions call for M1 increases, but you may use yarnover instead, creating an eyelet pattern at the two side edges. This shawl used one-half hank of yarn.

Knitting the Shawl

Cast on 3 stitches.

Row 1: Knit.

Row 2: Slip 1, K1, M1, knit to end of row.

Repeat Row 2 until shawl reaches desired size. Bind off loosely.

Crocheting the Optional Edging

With crochet hook, work 1 row of reverse single crochet around all edges.

Finishing

Weave in all ends. Wash shawl in warm water to soften the yarn, lay flat to dry.

Primitive Bag..............

This bag may look primitive, but it uses currently popular felting techniques and au courant novelty yarn to get that look. Embellished with bones and beads, no one will know you actually whipped it up yourself.

Photo, p. 101

MEASUREMENTS Approximately 7.5" (19 cm) wide and 13.5" (34.5 cm) tall with 30" (76 cm) handle, before felting, and approximately 4" (10 cm) wide and 4.75" (12 cm) tall with 20" (51 cm) handle, after felting (*Note:* Exact finished measurements will be determined by the yarn and the point at which you stop felting.)

YARN Brown Sheep, Lamb's Pride, 85% wool/15% mohair, 4 oz (113 g)/ 190 yds (174 m), M101 Sandy Heather

Norwegian Spirit (SandnesGarn), Funny, 100% polyester, 1.75 oz (50 g)/98 yds (90 m), small amount 3482 Chocolate, optional

NEEDLES US 15 (10 mm) straight needles or size you need to obtain correct gauge

GAUGE Approximately 8 stitches = 4" (10 cm) in garter stitch

OTHER SUPPLIES Crochet hook, beads, baubles, feathers, or other adornments

Designed by
Pat Taylor

Submitted by
Clickity Sticks & Yarns
Minneapolis, MN

Knitting the Bag

With Lamb's Pride, cast on 15 stitches.

Join Funny or use Lamb's Pride only and work garter stitch (knit every row) for 5 rows.

Drop Funny and work garter stitch with Lamb's Pride only for 12" more (about 48 rows).

Join Funny or use Lamb's Pride only and work garter stitch (knit every row) for 5 rows.

Assembling the Bag

Fold rectangle in half and sew side seams.

Knitting the Handle

Work 6-stitch I-cord (see Glossary, page 229) for 30".

Sew cord to the top of the bag at both sides.

Making the Closure

With crochet hook, make a chain approximately 1½ times longer than desired felted length; single crochet back along the chain.

Form a loop and sew it to the back of the bag.

Felting

Set the washer for the lowest water level, longest washing cycle, and hottest temperature. Add a small amount of detergent. Place bag in a zippered pillowcase and close. Place in machine with a pair of jeans or heavy towel to balance the load. Run on wash cycle only, checking felting status every 5 minutes. If necessary, reset the machine to wash cycle and agitate again. When desired effect is reached, run bag through cold rinse cycle to remove detergent, then through a spin cycle to remove excess water.

When bag is sufficiently felted, remove from washer and tug into shape. Dry flat or stuffed to shape.

Finishing

Sew on button or other object for loop closure.

Adorn as desired.

Photo, p. 116

Designed by
Gwen Steege
Williamstown, MA

Beaded Napkin Rings

A lovely sheen and a little sparkle are thanks to the linen/silk blend yarn and the simple crocheted edging accented with beads. If you've never worked with beads before, this is an easy and fun project to start with.

MEASUREMENTS Approximately 2.5" (6.5 cm) wide and 4.75" (12 cm) around

YARN Classic Elite Interlude, 30% silk/70% linen, 1.75 oz (50 g)/82 yds (75 m), 20266 Banana

NEEDLES	US 6 (4 mm) straight needles or size you need to obtain correct gauge
GAUGE	4.5 stitches = 1" (2.5 cm) in stockinette stitch
OTHER SUPPLIES	56 × ⅛" (3.5 mm) beads, one US G/6 (4.5 mm) crochet hook, tapestry needle

Knitting the Ring

Using waste yarn and a provisional method (see Glossary, page 232), cast on 10 stitches.

Row 1: With project yarn, P1, K1, P1, K4, P1, K1, P1.

Row 2: P1, K1, P6, K1, P1.

Repeat Rows 1 and 2 thirteen more times, or until piece measures approx 4.75", ending on Row 1. Cut yarn, leaving an 18" tail. Thread tail onto tapestry needle.

Remove waste yarn a stitch at a time and place the 10 stitches on a spare needle. With right sides of piece facing, bring together the ends of the ring and graft them closed using Kitchener Stitch (see Glossary, page 230).

Crocheting the Edging

String 14 beads onto the end of the ball of yarn.

Turn the knitted piece inside out, and with the wrong side facing you, crochet the edging as follows. *Note:* Work the crochet single chains in every other knit row.

Join yarn at the seam, ch 1, *sc in next 2 spaces, ch 1, pull up a bead and chain around it, ch 1, sc in the same space as the last sc; repeat from * to end of round; slip stitch into first ch1. Cut yarn and pull through last stitch. Repeat on other side of piece.

Make three more napkin rings.

Tip: To string small beads over thick yarn, thread a sewing needle with an 8-inch length of sewing thread; double the thread and tie the two ends together in a firm knot. Thread the pattern yarn through the loop of sewing thread, leaving a 10-inch tail. Draw the sewing needle through a bead, then pull the bead down the sewing thread and over the project thread.

Photo, p. 102

Submitted by
Clickity Sticks & Yarns
Minneapolis, MN

Flower Pin

You'll need 100% wool that felts easily for this project, but you can also knit in a strand of novelty yarn for highlights. These delightful flowers can be pinned to a lapel, attached to a hat, or used on pillows or curtain tiebacks — wherever you need a "little something." Each flower takes about 25 yards of wool.

MEASUREMENTS	Approximately 4.5" (11.5 cm) diameter (*Note:* Exact finished measurements will be determined by the yarn and the point at which you stop felting.)
YARN	100% wool, worsted weight, any brand
NEEDLES	Size US 7 (4.5 mm) straight needles or size you need to obtain correct gauge
GAUGE	16 stitches = 4" (10 cm) before felting
OTHER SUPPLIES	Tapestry needle, pin back (optional)

Getting Started

Cast on 5 stitches.

Knitting the Large Petals

Row 1: Kfb, K3, turn.

Row 2: P5.

Repeat Rows 1 and 2 four more times. You now have 10 stitches.

Row 11: K2tog, K4, turn.

Row 12: P5.

Repeat Rows 11 and 12 four more times. You now have 5 stitches. Do not bind off.

Repeat the sequence above twice more. You now have three large petals.

Knitting the Medium Petals

Begin these petals with the 5 stitches remaining from the last large petal.

Row 1: Ssk, K3.

Row 2: P4.

Row 3: Kfb, K2, turn.

Row 4: P4.

Repeat Rows 3 and 4 three more times. You now have 8 stitches.

Row 11: K2tog, K3, turn.

Row 12: P4.

Repeat Rows 11 and 12 three more times. You now have 4 stitches.

Repeat the sequence above, beginning with Row 3, three more times. You now have four medium petals.

Knitting the Small Petals

Begin these petals with the 4 stitches remaining from the last large petal.

Row 1: Ssk, K3.

Row 2: P3.

Row 3: Kfb, K1, turn.

Row 4: P3.

Repeat Rows 3 and 4 two more times. You now have 6 stitches.

Row 9: K2tog, K2, turn.

Row 10: P3.

Repeat Rows 9 and 10 two more times. You now have 3 stitches.

Repeat the sequence above, beginning with Row 3, two more times. You now have three small petals.

Bind off, leaving a 36" tail. Arrange petals as desired and sew them together with the tail. To make a stem, use remaining yarn to work 3-stitch I-cord (see Glossary, page 229) for 4". Weave in ends.

Felting the Flowers

Fill a washer with hot water at the lowest level. Place flowers in a zippered pillowcase and close. Place in washer with a pair of jeans or heavy towel to balance the load. Run machine on wash cycle only, checking felting status every 5 minutes. If necessary, reset the machine to wash cycle and agitate again. When desired effect is reached, wring out excess water and allow flowers to dry.

The Wave Hand Warmers

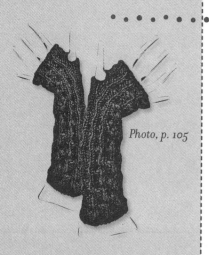

Photo, p. 105

Designed by
Jazmin Greenlaw

Submitted by
Webs
Northampton, MA

These fingerless mitts knitted in bulky yarn will work up quickly. Berkshire yarn is very soft and very, very warm. The mitts will keep your hands and wrists warm while leaving your fingers to work a keyboard or knit—whatever you fancy.

MEASUREMENTS   7.5" (19 cm) around at cuff and 10½" (26.5 cm) long

YARN   Valley Yarn, Berkshire, 85% wool/15% alpaca, 3.5 oz, (100 g)/ 108 yds (99 m), Plum

NEEDLES   Set of US 8 (5 mm) double-point needles or size you need to obtain correct gauge

GAUGE   16 stitches = 4" (10 cm) in stockinette stitch

Getting Started

Cast on 30 stitches and divide evenly onto three needles.

Mark beginning of round and join, being careful not to twist stitches.

Work 8-row Wave Pattern Stitch (see on facing page) six times (or to desired length).

Forming the Thumb Hole

Next Row: P2, K4, P2, bind off 4, *P2, K4; repeat from *.

Next Row: P2, K4, p2, cast on 4, *P2, K4; repeat from *.

Repeat pattern Row 1 two times.

Repeat pattern Row 5 four times.

Repeat Row 1 two times.

Bind off.

Finishing

Weave in ends. Block.

101

Have a Ball:
Sport-Weight Yarns

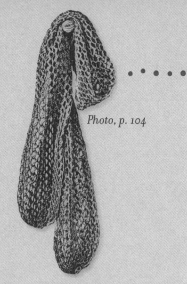

Designed by
Diana Foster

Submitted by
Lowellmountain Wools
Lowell, VT

Yarn Forward Over

Bring yarn to front of right needle, over to back, and between needles as if to purl.

Salmon Scarf

Here's another one of those great knitting patterns that look good from both sides. Knit one of these scarves in your favorite color. Then knit one in the color that looks best on you. Then knit one in your second-favorite color. Then knit one in your best friend's favorite color. And on and on!

MEASUREMENT 6" (15 cm) wide and 65" (165 cm) long

YARN Peace Fleece, 70% wool/30% mohair, 4 oz (113 g)/350 yds (320 m), Salmon

NEEDLES US 11 (8 mm) straight needles or size you need to obtain correct gauge

GAUGE 12 stitches = 4" (10 cm) in pattern

OTHER SUPPLIES Tapestry needle, two buttons

ABBREVIATIONS YFO Yarn forward over (see at left)

Knitting the Scarf

Cast on 18 stitches loosely.

Row 1: YFO, P2tog; repeat from *.

Repeat Row 1 until scarf measures 65" or desired length.

Bind off loosely.

Thread yarn on tapestry needle, gather up scarf ends, and secure.

Sew buttons to ends.

Variation

White scarf is worked exactly the same but with Tahki Cotton Classic, 100% cotton, 1.75 oz (50 g)/108 yds (99 m). Finished size is 5" × 56".

Purple Linen Pillow · · · · · · · · · · ·

One skein of this linen yarn sat in my stash for several months (or was that years?). When the idea of this one-skein book came into being, "pillow" became obvious. Both the Woven Basket Stitch used for the front and the garter stitch used for the back produced slightly openwork fabrics, so the pillow form underneath shows through. I covered my white form with a dark purple fabric before adding the knitted cover. The cover consumed all but 12 inches of my skein of yarn, so there is no room for variation. If you come up short on yarn, either make a single I-cord trim or eliminate the trim altogether.

Photo, p. 117

Designed by
Judith Durant
Lowell, MA

MEASUREMENT	To fit a 12" (30.5 cm) square pillow form
YARN	Louet Sales Euroflax, 100% linen, 4 oz (113 g)/325 yds (297 m), Eggplant
NEEDLES	US 5 (3.75 mm) straight needles and two US 5 (3.75 mm) double-point needles for I-cord or size you need to obtain correct gauge
GAUGE	32 stitches = 4" (10 cm) in Woven Basket Stitch; 20 stitches = 4" (10 cm) in garter stitch
OTHER SUPPLIES	12" × 12" pillow form, two pieces of fabric 13" × 13" to cover pillow (optional), tapestry needle
ABBREVIATIONS	CN Cable needle

Knitting the Pillow Front

Cast on 92 stitches. Work in Woven Basket Stitch (see at right) until piece measures approx 11" from beginning, ending on Row 5 of pattern. To keep cable crossing points from flaring out at the edge, reduce each 4-stitch cross to 2 stitches as follows: Slip 2 stitches to cable needle and hold in front, knit these stitches together with the next 2 stitches by K2tog 1 stitch from cable needle with 1 stitch from main needle, twice. Bind off on Row 7.

Woven Basket Stitch

Row 1 (wrong side): K2, *P4, K2; repeat from *.

Row 2: P2, *slip 2 stitches to cn and hold in back, K2, then K2 from cn, P2; repeat from *.

Row 3 and all other wrong-side rows: Knit the knits and purl the purls.

Row 4: P1, *slip 1 stitch to cn and hold in back, K2, P1 from cn; slip 2 stitches to cn and hold in front, P1, K2 from cn; repeat from * to last stitch, P1.

continued

Have a Ball: Sport-Weight Yarns

Row 6: P1, K2, P2, *slip 2 stitches to cn and hold in front, K2, K2 from cn, P2; repeat from * to last 3 stitches, K2, P1.

Row 8: P1, *slip 2 stitches to cn and hold in front, P1, K2 from cn; slip 1 stitch to cn and hold in back, K2, P1 from cn; repeat from * to last stitch, P1.

Repeat Rows 1–8 for pattern.

Photo, p. 119

Designed by
Kathryn Connelly

Submitted by
Hilltop Yarn
Seattle, WA

Knitting the Pillow Back

Cast on 52 stitches. Work in garter stitch (knit every row) until piece measures approx 11" from beginning. Bind off.

Pin front to back over pillow form. Thread tapestry needle with yarn and sew together the four edges.

Knitting the Trim

Work two pieces of 4-stitch I-cord (see Glossary, page 229) 48" long each. Twist the two cords around each other and sew the ends together. Pin in place evenly around pillow and use the rest of the yarn to stitch the cords in place on top of the joining seam.

Weave in all ends.

Yorkshire Tweed Beret

All you need to know to make this stylish beret is how to knit in the round. You begin at the brim, increase at six points to the widest part, then decrease down to the top center of the crown. Garter-stitch edging is attached to the provisional cast-on edge as it is knitted.

MEASUREMENT	Approximately 18.5" (47 cm) circumference
YARN	Rowan's Yorkshire Tweed DK, 100% wool, 1.75 oz (50 g)/124 yds (113 m), 342 Revel
NEEDLES	One US 7 (4.5 mm) circular needle 16" (40 cm) long and set of US 7 and 5 (4.5 and 3.75 mm) double-point needles or size you need to obtain correct gauge
GAUGE	18 stitches = 4" (10 cm) in stockinette stitch
OTHER SUPPLIES	Tapestry needle, size G/6 (4.5 mm) crochet hook, markers
ABBREVIATIONS	M1 Make 1 increase (see Glossary, page 231)

Getting Started

Cast on 84 stitches onto circular needle using provisional cast-on (see Glossary, page 232). Join into a round, being careful not to twist stitches.

Increasing

Round 1: Knit, placing markers every 14 stitches.

Round 2: Knit, slipping markers.

Round 3: *K14, M1, slip marker; repeat from *. You now have 90 stitches.

Round 4: Knit.

Round 5: *K15, M1, slip marker; repeat from *. You now have 96 stitches.

Round 6: Knit.

Continue in this manner, increasing 1 stitch before the marker every other round, until you have 126 stitches.

Knit 12 rounds even, or until piece measures 3.5" from beginning.

Decreasing

Round 1: *Knit to 2 stitches before maker, K2tog, slip marker; repeat from *. You now have 120 stitches.

Round 2: Knit.

Repeat Rounds 1 and 2, changing to larger double-point needles when necessary, until 66 stitches remain (11 stitches between each marker).

Work Round 1 only until 6 stitches remain.

Next Round: K2tog three times.

Work 3-stitch I-cord (see Glossary, page 229) for 6 rows. Break yarn, thread onto tapestry needle, and draw through remaining 3 stitches. Pull up snug and fasten off.

Knitting the Edging

Beginning at the end of the provisional cast-on, remove waste yarn and return stitches to circular needle.

Using the cable cast-on (see Glossary, page 228) and a single, smaller double-point needle, cast on 4 stitches at the beginning of the round.

Row 1: K3, ssk. (The ssk uses the fourth stitch from double-point needle and the next stitch from circular needle.

Row 2: Turn work. K4.

Repeat Rows 1 and 2 until all cast-on stitches are incorporated into the garter-stitch edging. Bind off 4 stitches.

Finishing

Sew 4-stitch seam at bottom edge.

Weave in all ends. Block.

Four-in-One Gaiter

This unisex design can be worn four different ways: neck warmer, face warmer, headband, or hat. Great for skiing, walking, or biking in winter. Go ahead and splurge on that extra-fine merino or that cashmere you've been eyeing—it takes only one skein!

MEASUREMENT	6.25" (16 cm) long and 11" (28 cm) around, unstretched; up to 22" (56 cm) around, stretched
YARN	Baruffa Maratona, 100% extra-fine merino, 1.75 oz (50 g)/121 yds (110 m), Color 8515
NEEDLE	One US 5 (3.75 mm) circular needle 16" (40 cm) long or size you need to obtain correct gauge
GAUGE	32 stitches = 4" (10 cm) in rib, unstretched
OTHER SUPPLIES	Stitch marker

Photo, p. 113

Designed by
Nancy Lindberg
Circle Pines, MN

Have a Ball: Sport-Weight Yarns

Knitting the Gaiter

Cast on 90 stitches.

Place marker and join into a round, being careful not to twist stitches.

Work K1, P1 rib for 6.25" or until skein almost runs out.

Bind off loosely. *Optional:* Bind off using larger needle.

Skinny Dipping:
Fingering-Weight Yarns

Adult and Child Socks

The hand-knitted-sock craze is not over, and with good reason! Socks are relatively quick to knit, and there are great yarns like this one from Cherry Tree Hill that are made especially for this purpose. If you've never worn hand-knitted socks before, it's time to start.

Designed by
Bernadette St. Amant

Submitted by
Clickity Sticks & Yarns
Minneapolis, MN

MEASUREMENTS	**Child:** 3" (7.5 cm) from top of cuff to top of heel, 6" (15 cm) from back of heel to end of toe
	Medium adult: 6" (15 cm) from top of cuff to top of heel, 8" (20.5 cm) from back of heel to end of toe
	Large adult: 7" (18 cm) from top of cuff to top of heel, 9" (23 cm) from back of heel to end of toe
YARN	Cherry Tree Hill Supersock, 100% merino wool, 4 oz (113 g)/420 yds (384 m), Winterberry
NEEDLES	Set of US 3 (3.25 mm) double-point needles or size you need to obtain correct gauge
GAUGE	30 stitches = 4" (10 cm) in stockinette stitch
OTHER SUPPLIES	Scrap yarn, tapestry needle

Child Sock

Knitting the Leg

Cast on 40 stitches loosely. Divide stitches evenly onto three needles as follows:

Needle 1	14 stitches
Needle 2	14 stitches
Needle 3	12 stitches

Join into a round, being careful not to twist stitches.

Work K1, P1 rib until piece measures 3" from top of cuff.

Knitting the Foot

Rib 20, knit 20 stitches with piece of scrap yarn. Knit the stitches that were just knitted with scrap yarn again, this time with working yarn.

Discontinue rib and work stockinette stitch only until sock measures 3" from scrap yarn or 2 inches less than finished length of foot.

Shaping the Toe

Round 1: K1, ssk, K14, K2tog, K2, ssk, K14, K2tog, K1.

Round 2: Knit.

Round 3: K1, ssk, K12, K2tog, K2, ssk, K12, K2tog, K1.

Round 4: Knit.

Continue in this manner, decreasing 4 stitches on every other round, until 16 stitches remain.

Divide remaining stitches evenly onto two needles with decreased edges on either end of needles. Cut yarn, leaving an 18" tail. Thread tail on tapestry needle and join toe with Kitchener Stitch (see Glossary, page 230).

Shaping the Heel

Slip the right leg of each stitch across top of scrap yarn onto a needle. Pick up 1 stitch in the corner. Slip the right leg of each stitch across bottom of scrap yarn onto another needle. Pick up 1 stitch in the corner. Distribute stitches evenly onto three needles and knit 1 row, knitting each picked-up stitch together with the stitch in front of it. You now have 40 stitches. Work decreases as for toe shaping.

When 14 stitches remain, divide remaining stitches evenly onto two needles, with decreased edges on either end of needles. Cut yarn, leaving an 18" tail. Thread tail on tapestry needle and join heel with Kitchener Stitch (see Glossary, page 230).

Adult Sock

Knitting the Leg

Cast on 56 (64) stitches loosely. Divide stitches evenly onto three needles:

Needle 1   18 (22) stitches

Needle 2   18 (22) stitches

Needle 3   20 (20) stitches

Join into a round, being careful not to twist stitches.

Work K2, P2 rib until cuff measures 6 (7)" from top of cuff.

Knitting the Foot

Rib 28 (32), knit 28 (32) with piece of scrap yarn. Knit the stitches that were just knitted with scrap yarn again, this time with working yarn.

Continue working K2, P2 rib on first half of stitches and stockinette on remaining 28 (32) stitches. Work even in established patterns until sock measures 5.5 (6.5)" from scrap yarn or 2" less than finished length of foot.

Shaping the Toe

Note: Maintain K2, P2 rib for top of sock.

Round 1: K1, ssk, rib 22 (26), K2tog, K2, ssk, K22 (26), K2tog, K1. You now have 52 (60) stitches.

Round 2: Rib the top stitches and knit the sole stitches.

Round 3: K1, ssk, rib 20 (24), K2tog, K2, ssk, K20 (24), K2tog, K1. You now have 48 (56) stitches.

Round 4: Rib the top stitches and knit the sole stitches.

Continue in this manner, decreasing 4 stitches on every other round, until 28 (32) stitches remain.

Divide remaining stitches evenly onto two needles, with decreased edges on either end of needles. Cut yarn, leaving an 18" tail. Thread tail on tapestry needle and join toe with Kitchener Stitch (see Glossary, page 230).

Shaping the Heel

Slip the right leg of each stitch across top of scrap yarn onto a needle. Pick up 1 stitch in the corner. Slip the right leg of each stitch across bottom of scrap yarn onto another needle. Pick up 1 stitch in the corner. Distribute stitches evenly onto three needles and knit 1 row, knitting each picked-up stitch together with the stitch in front of it. You now have 56 (64) stitches. Work decreases as for toe shaping.

When 28 (32) stitches remain, divide remaining stitches evenly onto two needles, with decreased edges on either end of needles. Cut yarn, leaving an 18" tail. Thread tail onto tapestry needle and join heel with Kitchener Stitch (see Glossary, page 230).

Finishing

Weave in ends. Block.

Curly Curtain Tiebacks ·········

Knitted wool tiebacks look great with velvet and other heavy curtains. These have a twisted cable pattern and corkscrew fringe. The pair used only 35 of the 50 grams in the skein, so you could make them longer or wider if desired.

Photo, p. 108

Designed by
Judith Durant
Lowell, MA

MEASUREMENTS	Approximately 18" (45.5 cm) long and 1.5" (4 cm) wide
YARN	Koigu Premium Merino, 100% merino wool, 1.75 oz (50 g)/175 yds (160 m), Color 1019
NEEDLES	US 3 (3.25 mm) straight needles or size you need to obtain correct gauge
GAUGE	8 stitches = 1" (2.5 cm) in stockinette stitch
OTHER SUPPLIES	4 × ½" (1.3 cm) plastic rings, 1.5 yd (114 cm) 1½" (4 cm) wide grosgrain ribbon

Skinny Dipping: Fingering-Weight Yarns

Stitch Pattern

Rows 1 and 5: Knit.

Rows 2, 4, and 6: K3, P6, K3.

Row 3: K4, skip 2 stitches and knit next 2 stitches from behind, leaving them on the needle, knit the 2 skipped stitches and drop the 2 previously knitted stitches from the needle, K4.

Repeat Rows 1–6 for pattern.

Knitting the Tiebacks (make 2)

Cast on 12 stitches. Knit 6 rows.

Work the 6-row Stitch Pattern (see at left) until piece measures 18" or desired length.

Knit 6 rows.

Knitting the Curly Fringe

Bind off 3 stitches. Keeping remaining stitch from bind-off on needle, place remaining 8 stitches on a holder.

*Using the knitted-on method, cast on 29 stitches. You now have 30 stitches.

Knit into the front and back of every stitch. You now have 60 stitches.

Purl 1 row.

Bind off 59 stitches. Keeping remaining stitch from bind-off on right needle, place next 2 stitches nearest fringe from holder on left needle. Bind off 2 stitches.

Repeat from * for three more fringes.

Cut yarn. Draw tail through last stitch on needle.

Finishing

Weave in ends. Twist the fringes around your finger to make them curl. Block, omitting fringes. Hand- or machine-stitch grosgrain ribbon to back, sew rings to ends. *Optional:* Crochet over the rings with yarn before attaching them to the tiebacks.

Sequin Barrette············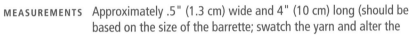·····

Photo, p. 103

Designed by
Nancy Miller

Submitted by
KnitWit Yarn Shop
Portland, ME

This is a classic barrette that goes with everything. One ball of yarn yields three barrettes of this size: a terrific way to use up several favorite yarns when you don't have full skeins.

MEASUREMENTS	Approximately .5" (1.3 cm) wide and 4" (10 cm) long (should be based on the size of the barrette; swatch the yarn and alter the pattern as necessary)
YARN	Trendsetter Can-Can, 80% cotton/20% PVC, .35 oz (10 g)/32 yds (30 m), black/silver
NEEDLES	US 1 (2.25mm) straight needles or size you need to obtain correct gauge
GAUGE	Approximately 10 stitches = 1" (2.5 cm) in stockinette stitch

Knitting the Barrette

Cast on 10 stitches, leaving a 6" tail.

Knit in stockinette stitch (knit 1 row, purl 1 row) for the length of the barrette plus 1".

Finishing

Bind off. Wrap long sides to back of barrette and use tails from cast-on and bind-off to sew the knitting onto the back of the barrette.

Designed by
Leah Oakley

Submitted by
Haus of Yarn
Nashville, TN

Handpaint Highlights Socks

This pattern is written specifically for hand-painted or hand-dyed yarns. It's designed to pull out the beautiful highlights of the yarn, and you can get a pair of small or medium women's socks out of a 100-gram skein. So go ahead and buy that lovely hand-painted yarn you saw last week—it takes only one skein!

MEASUREMENTS	**Woman's small:** 5" (12.5 cm) from top of cuff to top of heel, 9" (23 cm) from back of heel to end of toe
	Woman's medium: 5" (12.5 cm) from top of cuff to top of heel, 9.5" (24 cm) from back of heel to end of toe
YARN	Mountain Colors Bearfoot, 100% wool, 3.5 oz (100 g)/350 yds (320 m), Bitterroot Rainbow
NEEDLES	Set of US 1 (2.25 mm) double-point needles or size you need to obtain correct gauge
GAUGE	32 stitches = 4" (10 cm) in pattern
OTHER SUPPLIES	Three markers (one green, one red, one other color for end of round)
ABBREVIATION	EOR End of round

Knitting the Cuff

Cast on 60 (72) stitches. Divide the stitches evenly among three needles (20 [24] each), place EOR marker, and join into a round, being careful not to twist the stitches.

Knit K1, P1 rib until piece measures 1.25" from beginning.

Knitting the Leg

Work Slipped Handpaint Rib Pattern (see facing page) until piece measures 5" from beginning and ending after completing Round 1 of pattern.

Knitting the Heel Flap

Knit 2 stitches from Needle 1 (2 stitches past EOR marker) to Needle 3. Leave the remaining 18 (22) stitches on Needle 1 and slip 10 (12) stitches from Needle 2 to Needle 1. These 28 (34) stitches will be held for the instep.

At this point, you will be working on the back 32 (38) stitches only. Remove EOR marker when you come to it.

Turn work so wrong side is facing. Work back and forth over 32 (38) heel flap stitches as follows:

Row 1 (wrong side): *Sl 1 wyif, K1; repeat from * to last 2 stitches, Sl 1, P1.

Row 2 (right side): Sl 1 wyib, *K1 tbl, P1; repeat from * to last stitch, K1.

Repeat Rows 1 and 2 for 2½" and end after completing Row 2.

Turning the Heel

Beginning on a wrong-side row, turn the heel as follows:

Slip 1, P16 (20), P2tog, P1, turn.

Slip 1, K5, ssk, K1, turn.

Slip 1, P6, P2tog, P1, turn.

Slip 1, K7, ssk, K1, turn.

Slip 1, P8, P2tog, P1, turn.

Slip 1, K9, ssk, K1, turn.

Continue in this manner, working one more stitch before the decrease in each row, ending after completing a right-side row. You now have 20 (22) stitches.

Knitting the Gusset

With right side facing you, pick up and knit into each slipped stitch along one edge of the heel flap. Place green marker, then begin working the 28 (34) instep stitches that have been on hold in established pattern as follows:

K1, P1, work Round 2 of Slipped Handpaint Rib Pattern over 24 (32) stitches, K2 (0). Place red marker.

Slipped Handpaint Rib Pattern

Note: Slip all stitches purlwise.

Rounds 1–3: *K3, P1; repeat from *.

Round 4: *K2, yo, K1, P1; repeat from *.

Round 5: *K1, sl 1 wyib, drop yo from previous round, K1, P1; repeat from *.

Round 6: *K1, sl 1 wyib, K1, P1; repeat from *.

Repeat Round 1–6 for pattern.

Pick up and knit into each slipped stitch along the other edge of the heel flap, making sure you pick up the same number of stitches you did for the first side. Knit 10 (11) stitches and place EOR marker.

Work gusset as follows (you will begin with Round 3 of pattern).

For small size:

Round 1: Knit to 3 stitches before green marker, K2tog, K1, slip marker, K1, P1, work in pattern to 2 stitches before red marker, K2, slip marker, K1, ssk, knit to end of round.

Round 2: Knit to green marker, slip marker, K1, P1, work in pattern to 2 stitches before red marker, K2, slip marker, knit to end of round.

For medium size:

Round 1: Knit to 3 stitches before green marker, K2tog, K1, slip marker, K1, P1, work in pattern to red marker, slip marker, K1, ssk, knit to end of round.

Round 2: Knit to green marker, slip marker, K1, P1, work in pattern to red marker, slip marker, knit to end of round.

Repeat Rounds 1 and 2 until you have your original number of stitches— 60 (72) stitches.

Knitting the Foot

Knit to green marker, K1, P1, work in pattern over 26 (34) instep stitches, K2 (0), slip red marker, knit to end of round.

Continue in this manner until foot is 1.5" (1.75") shorter than desired finished length, removing green and red markers on the last round.

Next Round: Slip EOR marker, K15 (18), place green marker, K30 (36), place red marker, knit to end of round.

Shaping the Toe

Round 1: Knit to 3 stitches before green marker, K2tog, K1, slip marker, K1, ssk, knit to 3 stitches before red marker, K2tog, k1, slip marker, K1, ssk, knit to end of round.

Round 2: Knit.

Repeat Rounds 1 and 2 until 32 (40) stitches remain.

Repeat Round 1 only until 16 (20) stitches remain.

Knit to green marker.

Place 4 (5) stitches before and after EOR marker on one needle, removing the marker.

Place remaining 8 (10) stitches on another needle.

Graft toe stitches together using the Kitchener Stitch (see Glossary, page 230).

Finishing

Weave in ends. Block.

Heart Pin······················

Now you can proudly wear your heart on your shirt-sleeve—or your lapel, or your hat, or your handbag, just about anywhere else you want. And since each one takes only 7½ yards, you can crochet hearts to wear in many places from just one small ball of perle cotton.

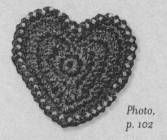

Photo, p. 102

MEASUREMENTS	Approximately 1.75" (4.5 cm) wide, 1.75" (4.5 cm) deep
YARN	DMC Perle Cotton #5, 100% cotton, .3 oz (10 g)/52 yds (48 m), Color 321
NEEDLE	One #6 (1.6 mm) steel crochet hook
OTHER SUPPLIES	45 size 11/0 Delica 2-cut beads in galvanized silver, beading needle

Designed by
Leanne Walker

Submitted by
KnitWit Yarn Shop
Portland, ME

Getting Started

Thread beads onto yarn (see pages 158–159). The beads will be used in the final round only, so just keep pushing them down the yarn until you need them.

Ch 4, join into a ring with a slip stitch.

Skinny Dipping: Fingering-Weight Yarns

Crocheting the Heart

Round 1: Ch 2, 11 sc in ring, join with slip stitch to top of ch2. You now have 12 spaces in which to work.

Round 2: Begin to shape circle into a heart. Ch 2 (counts as hdc), 4 dc in next space, hdc in next space, slip stitch across next space, hdc in next space, 4 dc in next space, hdc in next space, sc in next 2 spaces, hdc, 2 dc and another hdc in next space, 2 sc in each of next 2 spaces, join with slip stitch to top of ch2.

Round 3: Ch 3, dc in next 2 spaces, 6 dc in next space, sc next space, sl st in each of next 3 spaces, sc in next space, 6 dc in next space, dc in next 3 spaces, hdc in next 3 spaces, 2 dc in next space, 2 triple crochet in next space (this is tip of heart bottom), 2 dc next space, hdc next 3 spaces, join with slip stitch to top of ch3.

Round 4: Ch 3, dc in each of next 4 spaces, 2dc in each of next 3 spaces, hdc in each of next 3 spaces, skip one space, sl st in next space (this is top of heart between the two bumps), skip one space, hdc in each of next 3 spaces, 2 dc in each of next 3 sp, 1 dc in each of next 5 spaces, 1 hdc in each of next 4 spaces, 2 sc next space, 3 hdc in next space, 2 sc in each of next two spaces, hdc in each of next 3 spaces, join with slip stitch to top of ch3.

Round 5: Ch 2, sc in each of next 6 stitches, 2 sc in each of next 4 spaces, sc each of next 3 spaces, sl st across next 2 spaces, sc in each of next 3 spaces, 2 sc in each of next 4 spaces, sc in each of next 12 spaces, 2 sc in each of next 3 spaces, sc in each of next 5 spaces, join with slip stitch to top of ch2.

Round 6: Turn piece over to wrong side (to ensure that the beads appear on the front of the pin). Work reverse sc around edge evenly spaced, sliding a bead down on final part of each rev sc (when pulling the final loop through the 2 loops on the hook to complete the stitch).

Finishing

Weave in ends. Sew pin to back.

Fabulous Filigree Scarf……………

The instructions for this fabulous scarf look more complicated than they actually are. Once you get into the rhythm of working first one half, then the other, you'll find the knitting quite meditative.

MEASUREMENTS	Center back neck to back point 12" (30.5 cm), center back neck to front point 18" (46 cm)
YARN	Dale of Norway Baby Ull, 100% machine-washable wool, 1.75 oz (50 g)/180 yds (165 m), 4018 Red
NEEDLES	US 6 (4 mm) straight needles or size you need to obtain correct gauge
GAUGE	16 stitches = 4" (10 cm) in pattern, blocked
OTHER SUPPLIES	One black and one red stitch marker; tapestry needle, pin for closure
ABBREVIATION	WT Wrap, turn (see at right)

Getting Started

You will need to work with two strands of yarn when working tails, so either wind a center-pull ball so you can work with both ends or wind about one-quarter of the yarn into a second ball.

Using the provisional method (see Glossary, page 232), cast on 7 stitches.

Set-up Row: Knit.

Knitting the Point

Row 1: K4, K2tog WT. You now have 6 stitches.

Row 2: K4, Kfb. You now have 7 stitches.

Row 3: K5, WT.

Row 4: K4, Kfb. You now have 8 stitches.

Row 5: K5, WT.

Row 6: K4, Kfb. You now have 9 stitches.

Photo, p. 110

Designed by
Margaret Anne Halas

Submitted by
Sew Krazy
Wooster, OH

Short Rows

Short rows require a maneuver called WT, wrap and turn. Wrapping a stitch prevents a hole from forming at the turn. Bring yarn to front, slip next stitch purlwise, bring yarn to back, slip the stitch back to left needle, turn work, and work next row.

Skinny Dipping: Fingering-Weight Yarns

Row 7: K8, WT.

Row 8: K6, K2tog. You now have 8 stitches.

Row 9: K4, WT.

Row 10: K2, K2tog. You now have 7 stitches.

Row 11: K4, WT.

Row 12: K2, K2tog. You now have 6 stitches.

Row 13: Knit 6.

Working the Pickup Row

Carefully slip the 6 loops of main color from provisional cast-on onto free needle, starting at the end farthest from the point of the needle left in the work. Do not knit these stitches; simply slip them onto the needle.

Pull out scrap yarn, carefully removing provisional cast-on stitches. You have 6 stitches already knitted on the right needle and the 6 you just picked up, on the left needle, ready to knit.

To finish the row, place black marker, yo, place red marker, work Row 1 of Lace Chart (see page 189) over remaining 6 stitches. You now have 15 stitches on needle: 6 stitches, marker, yo, marker, 8 stitches.

Next Row (wrong side of center section): Work Row 2 of lace chart to red marker. Slip red marker, knit to black marker, slip black marker, work Row 1 of lace chart. Turn work and work Row 2 of lace pattern to black marker.

You have now completed one "cycle" — you worked Rows 1 and 2 of the lace pattern on each side of the center section and are ready to go to the next cycle, knitting Rows 3 and 4 from lace chart.

Knitting the Main Body

Row 1 (right side): On rows where the center section starts with the black marker, work the even-numbered lace row that was worked at the beginning of the previous row, slip black marker, yarnover, knit to red marker, yarnover, slip red marker, work odd-numbered row from chart.

Row 2 (wrong side): On rows where the center section starts with the red marker, work next even-numbered lace row to marker, slip red marker, knit to black marker, slip black marker, work the odd-numbered lace row that was worked at the end of the previous row.

Continue knitting the 8-row lace pattern in this manner, increasing with yarnovers on right side rows as established, until there are 75 stitches between the markers and ending after completing a row with wrong side of the center section.

Dividing for the Tails

Next Row (right side): Work Row 4 of lace pattern to black marker, slip marker, yo, K25, bind off 25, knit to red marker, yo, slip marker, work Row 5 of lace pattern. You now have 26 stitches (25 plus yo) on each side, plus the lace edge stitches.

Next Row (wrong side): Work Row 6 of lace pattern to red marker, slip marker, knit to end of side. Attach second strand of yarn to beginning of second side of scarf. Knit to black marker, slip marker, work Row 5 of lace pattern.

Knitting the Tails

Note: Do not put down your work with one tail on each needle—always finish working across both tails.

Row 1:

Right Tail (right side) Work appropriate even-numbered row of lace pattern to black marker, slip marker, yo, work to within 6 stitches of end, K3tog, K3.

Left Tail (right side) K3, (Sl 2, K1, P2sso), knit to red marker, yo, slip marker, work appropriate odd-numbered row of lace pattern.

Row 2:

Left Tail (wrong side) Work appropriate even-numbered row of lace pattern to red marker, slip marker, knit to end.

Right Tail (wrong side) Knit to black marker, slip marker, work appropriate odd-numbered row of lace pattern.

Repeat these 2 rows until 5 stitches remain between neck edge and markers, ending after completing a wrong-side row.

Knitting the Tail Ends

Continue working across both tails.

Row 1:

Right Tail Work Row 8 of lace to black marker, slip marker, yo, K3tog, K2.

Left Tail K2, (Sl 2, K1, P2sso), yo, slip marker, work Row 1 of lace.

Row 2:

Left Tail Work Row 2 of lace, slip red marker, K4.

Right Tail K4, slip black marker, work Row 1 of lace.

Row 3:

Right Tail Work Row 2 of lace to black marker, slip marker, yo, K3tog, K1.

Left Tail K1, (Sl 2, K1, P2sso), yo, slip marker, work Row 3 of lace.

Row 4:

Left Tail Work Row 4 of lace, slip red marker, K3.

Right Tail K3, slip black marker, work Row 3 of lace.

Row 5:

Right Tail Work Row 4 of lace to black marker, slip marker, yo, K3tog.

Left Tail (Sl 2, K1, P2sso), yo, slip marker, work Row 5 of lace.

Row 6:

Left Tail Work Row 6 of lace, slip red marker, K2.

Right Tail K2, slip black marker, work Row 5 of lace.

Row 7:

Right Tail Work Row 6 of lace to black marker, slip marker, K2tog.

Left Tail K2tog, remove red marker, work Row 7 of lace.

Row 8:

Left Tail Bind off 6, K4, K2tog.

Right Tail K1, remove black marker, work Row 7 of lace.

Row 9:

Right Tail Bind off 6, K4, K2tog.

Working the End Points

Work both the same, one at a time.

Row 1: K6.

Row 2: K5, WT.

Row 3: K5.

Row 4: K4, WT.

Row 5: K4.

Row 6: K3, WT.

Row 7: K3.

Row 8: K2, WT.

Row 9: K2.

Row 10: K1, WT.

Row 11: K1.

Bind off.

Finishing

Weave in ends. Block.

Lace Chart

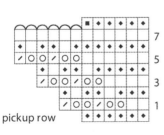

pickup row

Key

☐	knit odd # rows ; purl even # rows
◆	knit even-numbered rows
○	yarn over
╱	K2tog
⌒	bind off
■	last bound-off st on needle

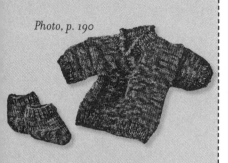

Designed by
Jean Austin

Submitted by
Craftique/Never
Enough Knitting
Wheaton, IL

"Orphan" Sweater and Socks

Made from a leftover ball of sock yarn (known as an "orphan"), this short-sleeved sweater and matching socks are sized to fit 18" (46 cm) dolls.

MEASUREMENTS	To fit dolls 14" (35.5 cm) chest and 18" (46 cm) tall
YARN	Patons Kroy Socks, 75% wool/25% nylon, 1.75 oz (50 g)/203 yds (186 m), 54561 Winter Eclipse
NEEDLES	US 2 (2.75 mm) straight needles and set of US 2 (2.75 mm) double-point needles or size you need to obtain correct gauge
GAUGE	30 stitches = 4" (10 cm) in stockinette stitch
ABBREVIATIONS	WT wrap and turn (see facing page)

"Orphan" Sweater

Knitting the Sweater Back

With straight needles, cast on 52 stitches. Beginning with a wrong-side row, work 7 rows of K1, P1 rib.

Change to stockinette stitch and work even until piece measures 6" from beginning, ending with a wrong-side row.

Bind off 13 stitches at the beginning of the next 2 rows.

Place remaining 26 stitches on holder.

Knitting the Sweater Front

Work as for back until piece measures 5" from beginning.

Left Front

Row 1: K16, K2tog, turn.

Row 2: Purl.

Row 3: K to last 2 stitches, K2tog, turn.

Row 4: Purl.

Repeat Rows 3 and 4 until 13 stitches remain.

Work even in stockinette stitch until piece measures same as back.

Bind off remaining 13 left front stitches.

Place 16 stitches on holder for neck.

Right Front

Join yarn.

Row 1: K2tog tbl, knit to end of row.

Row 2: Purl.

Repeat Rows 1 and 2 until 13 stitches remain.

Work even in stockinette stitch until piece measures same as back.

Knitting the Sleeves (make 2)

Cast on 36 stitches. Beginning with a wrong-side row, work K1, P1 rib for 5 rows.

Change to stockinette stitch and work even until piece measures 2" from beginning.

Bind off loosely.

Assembling the Sweater

Join shoulder seams with three-needle bind-off (see Glossary, page 235).

Measure down 2.5" from shoulder seam on all sides and mark. Spread sweater pieces flat and center the sleeves at shoulder seams. Sew together with back stitch between the marks.

Sew side seams.

Wrap and Turn (WT)

To wrap and turn on a knit row, bring yarn forward, slip the next stitch onto right needle, bring yarn to back. Leave the wrapped stitch on right needle and turn.

To wrap and turn on a purl row, bring yarn to back, slip the next stitch onto right needle, bring yarn to front. Leave the wrapped stitch on right needle and turn.

Knitting the Neck Edge

With double-point needles, begin at left front neck edge and pick up and knit 9 stitches along left front edge, knit 16 front neck stitches from holder, pick up and knit 9 stitches along right front edge, knit 26 back neck stitches from holder. Divide 60 stitches onto three double-point needles, 20 stitches each.

Work K1 P1 rib for 7 rounds.

Bind off loosely. Weave in ends.

"Orphan" Socks

Knitting the Leg

With double-point needles, cast on 30 stitches and divide evenly onto three needles, 10 stitches each.

Work K1, P1 rib for 5 rounds.

Change to stockinette stitch and knit 8 rounds.

Knitting the Heel Flap

Work the heel on the 10 stitches on Needle 1 only.

Row 1: *Sl 1, K1; repeat from *.

Row 2: *Sl 1, purl; repeat from *.

Repeat these two rows twice more for a total of 6 rows worked.

Turning the Heel

Row 1: K5, K2tog tbl, K1, turn.

Row 2: Sl 1, P3, P2og, P1, turn.

Row 3: Sl 1, K4, K2tog tbl, K1, turn.

Row 4: Sl 1, P3, P2tog, P1. You now have 6 stitches.

Knitting the Gusset

Knit 6 stitches on Needle 1 and with same needle pick up and knit 5 stitches along side of heel.

With new needle, knit 10 stitches from Needle 2 and 10 stitches from Needle 3.

With new needle, pick up and knit 5 stitches along side of heel and knit 3 stitches from Needle 1.

You have 8 stitches on Needle 1, 20 stitches on Needle 2, and 8 stitches on Needle 3.

Finishing the Sole

Each WT (see sidebar, page 191) will move one stitch from Needle 2 onto Needle 1 or Needle 3. (Leave the remaining stitches on Needle 2 behind when you turn to work back on either Needle 1 or Needle 3.)

Needle 1 Knit to 2 stitches from end, K2tog. WT one stitch from Needle 2. Sl 1 (wrapped stitch), purl to end.

Needle 3 Purl to end, WT one stitch from Needle 2. Sl 1 (wrapped stitch), K2tog tbl, knit to end.

Repeat these two needle instructions until 10 stitches remain on Needle 2.

Return to knitting in the round.

Needle 1 Knit to 2 stitches, K2tog.

Needle 2 Knit.

Needle 3 K2tog tbl, knit to end.

Repeat these three needle instructions until 20 stitches remain.

Knit 5 rounds.

Shaping the Toe

Needle 1 Knit to 2 stitches, K2tog.

Needle 2 K2tog tbl, knit to last 2 stitches, K2tog.

Needle 3 K2tog tbl, knit to end.

Repeat these three needle instructions once more. You now have 12 stitches.

Photo, p. 119

Designed by
Judith Durant
Lowell, MA

Lace Pattern

Worked over a multiple of 3 stitches plus 4.

Row 1: K2, *slip 1, K2tog, psso, yo twice; repeat from * to last 2 stitches, K2.

Row 2: K2, *P1, K1 into double yo, P1; repeat from * to last 2 stitches, K2.

Row 3: Knit.
Repeat Rows 1–3 for pattern.

With Needle 3, knit stitches from Needle 1. You now have 6 stitches on each of two needles. Graft these 12 stitches together with Kitchener Stitch (see Glossary, page 230).

Finishing

Weave in ends. Block.

Red Hot Necklace

The viscose in this yarn is shiny, and it cried out to be paired with beads. The stitch pattern is worked over a multiple of 3 plus 4 stitches, so you can knit to any width. The pattern also has a three-row repeat—it looks the same on both sides, making it ideal for this wrap-style necklace.

MEASUREMENTS	Approximately 2" (5 cm) wide and 58" (147.5 cm) long, before adding tassels
YARN	Sesia Isa, 55% cotton/45% viscose, 1.75 oz (50 g)/160 yds (146 m), Color 201
NEEDLES	US 3 (3.25 mm) straight needles or size you need to obtain correct gauge
GAUGE	13 stitches = 2" (5 cm) in pattern
OTHER SUPPLIES	2 focal beads, 192 size 6/0 pony beads, 12 × 7 mm round beads, and 12 size 11/0 seed beads; beading needle, nylon beading thread

Knitting the Necklace

Cast on 13 stitches.

Work in Lace Pattern (see at left) until piece measures 58" or desired length, ending with Row 2 of pattern.

Bind off.

Adding the Fringe

Use cast-on and bind-off tails to gather ends of necklace, and make a small loop of yarn at the center of each end.

With threaded beading needle, tie tail around loop and string beads as follows.

Focal bead, *16 pony beads, one 7 mm bead, and one seed bead; pass back through 7 mm bead, pony beads, and focal bead; pass thread around loop. Pass through focal bead and repeat from * five more times. Fasten off thread and bury tail. Weave in ends.

Sachet ·

Fill this sachet with your favorite scent and place in your lingerie drawer or in your sweater storage box. Fill with potpourri, fancy soap shavings, or perfume saturated cotton balls. Tiny as it is, go ahead and make a bunch for you and yours.

Designed by
Dorothy T. Ratigan
Cape Elizabeth, ME

Photo, p. 106

MEASUREMENTS	3" (7.5 cm) wide and 2.25" (5.5) tall
YARN	DMC Coton Perle #5, 100% cotton, .3 oz (10 g)/52 yd (48 m), 966 Medium Baby Green
NEEDLE	One US B/1 (2 mm) crochet hook
GAUGE	Approximately 7 hdc = 1" (2.5 cm)
OTHER SUPPLIES	98 size 8/0 beads; beading needle; ½ yd (45.5 cm) ⅛" (3 mm) double-sided satin ribbon
ABBREVIATIONS	hdc half double crochet (see Glossary, page 228) sb slide bead against last stitch

Crocheting the Sachet

Using beading needle, thread beads onto yarn (see page 159 for stringing tip).

Ch 23, skip first ch and work 1 hdc in each chain. You made 22 hdc. Ch 1, turn.

Row 1: 3 hdc, sb, *2 hdc, sb; repeat from * to last 3 stitches, 3 hdc. Ch 1, turn.

Row 2: Work 22 hdc. Ch 1, turn.

Row 3: 4 hdc, sb, *2 hdc, sb; repeat from * to last 4 stitches, 4 hdc. Ch 1, turn.

Row 4: Repeat Row 2.

Repeat Rows 1–4 five more times, then repeat Rows 1 and 2.

Work one row slip stitch. Slip-stitch side seams together.

Cut yarn, weave in ends.

Starting at center front, thread the ribbon under 2 hdc and over 2 hdc back to center front. Fill the sachet as desired. Tie a bow in the ribbon.

Floral Mesh Shawl

This shawl is shaped like a square with an opening from one of the corners to the center; it is guaranteed to stay on your shoulders! Knitted in a multicolored silk, it is as lightweight as it is luscious.

MEASUREMENTS	Approximately 40" (101.5 cm) square
YARN	Schaefer Andrea, 100% silk, 3.5 oz (100 g)/1093 yds (1000 m), Mary Breckinridge
NEEDLES	One 3 mm circular needle 24" (60 cm) long and set of four 3 mm double-point needles or size you need to obtain correct gauge
GAUGE	32 stitches= 4" (10 cm) in pattern
OTHER SUPPLIES	Stitch markers

Photo, p. 106

Designed by
Catherine Devine

Submitted by
Knitting, Etc.
Ithaca, NY

Skinny Dipping: Fingering-Weight Yarns

Knitting the Neckband

Using a smooth yarn in a contrasting color and a short double-point needle, provisionally cast on 7 stitches (see Glossary, page 232).

Set-up Row: P1, (K1, P1) three times.

Note: Slipping the first stitch of each row creates a neat chain-stitch edge.

Row 1 (right side): Slip 1, (K1, P1) three times, slip 1, (P1, K1) three times.

Row 2: Slip 1, (P1, K1) three times, slip 1, (K1, P1) three times.

Repeat Rows 1 and 2 until you have 72 loops along the edge of the strip, ending with a wrong-side row.

Setting Up for the Body

With right side facing and using circular needle, begin at the bottom of neckband and pick up the 72 loops on the left edge, inserting the needle through each loop from back to front.

Slide the 7 live stitches at the end of the neckband onto the circular needle.

Slip 1, (K1, P1) three times across the ribbing stitches, turn. Slip 1 (P1, K1) three times back across the ribbing stitches. Slip 1 (K1, P1) two times, K1, place marker, purl the last rib stitch with first loop on circular needle. (These extra rows will allow the ribbing to turn the corner from the neckband to the front band.)

You will now be working along the picked-up stitches of the neckband.

Knit the 71 remaining picked-up neckband stitches through the back loop, placing a marker after the 18th, 36th, and 54th stitches. Place the 7 stitches from the provisional cast-on onto a double-point needle and remove the waste yarn. Purl 1, (K1, P1) three times across the picked-up stitches. Slip 1 (P1, K1) three times, turn. Slip 1 (K1, P1) three times back to the outside edge. Slip 1 (P1, K1) two times, P1, place marker, knit the last rib stitch together with the first of the 72 neckband stitches to make the first stitch of chart row 1 (see Floral Mesh Shawl Chart, page 198.

Knitting the Lace

The chart represents one-quarter of the body stitches and is worked four times between the previously placed markers, while keeping the first and last

6 stitches in ribbing. Only the right-side rows are charted; for all wrong-side rows, purl all stitches between the ribbings. Work all 48 rows of the chart three times, then work through Row 14.

Knitting the Edging

Using double-point needles and working only the 6 rib stitches, slip 1, (P1, K1) two times, P1, turn. Slip 1, (P1, K1) two times, P1, turn. Slip 1, (P1, K1) two times, purl the last rib stitch with 1 stitch from the shawl body.

Work back to the outside edge. Now continue the ribbing, knitting the last rib stitch of each row with 1 stitch from the shawl body. Repeat the extra rows at the next three corners. At the other front edge, work the extra row after the last stitch of the shawl body. Graft or knit together the two ends of the band.

Blocking the Shawl

Dampen the shawl on both sides by misting it with a spray bottle filled with plain water. Pin the shawl out to about 40" square, overlapping the front bands. Let dry thoroughly.

Floral Mesh Shawl Chart

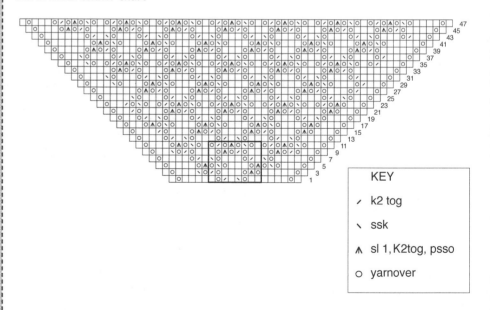

KEY

✓ k2 tog

╲ ssk

⋀ sl 1, K2tog, psso

○ yarnover

Lace Bookmark · · · · · · · · · · · · ·

This lace bookmark is a nice way to add a little romance to your reading. But feel free to use one in your mystery novel or biography, too, because you can make three bookmarks out of just one skein of perle cotton.

Photo, p. 112

MEASUREMENTS   Approximately 1" (2.5 cm) wide and 7" (18 cm) long

YARN   DMC Perle Coton #5, 100% cotton, .35 oz (10 g), 52 yds (48 m), 341 Light Blue Violet

NEEDLES   US 1 (2.25 mm) straight needles or size you need to obtain correct gauge

GAUGE   Approximately 10 stitches = 1" (2.5 cm) in pattern

OTHER SUPPLIES   3 × 4 mm bicone crystals; 52 each size 11/0 cut cylinder beads in blue and silver; spray starch

Designed by
Nancy Miller

Submitted by
KnitWit Yarn Shop
Portland, ME

Knitting the Bookmark

Cast on 9 stitches, leaving a 6" tail.

Row 1: K2tog, K2, yo, K1, yo, K2, K2tog.

Rows 2, 4, and 6: Purl.

Row 3: K2tog, K1, yo, K3, yo, K1, K2tog.

Row 5: K2tog, yo, K5, yo, K2tog.

Repeat Rows 1–6 eleven more times, ending on Row 5 of pattern. Bind off in purl.

Finishing

Weave in end. Spray with starch. With waxed thread attached to end of bookmark, string beads to make fringe. I alternated blue and silver with a crystal on the end.

101

Variety Is the Spice of Life:
Novelty Yarns

Designed by
Alexandra Immel

Submitted by
Hilltop Yarn
Seattle, WA

Knitted Coasters with Charms

These colorful and beaded coasters make great gifts. You'll like knitting them so much that you'll want to make a set for everyone you know.

MEASUREMENTS	Approximately 4" (10 cm) square or 5" (12.5 cm) square
YARN	Noro Daria, 55% cotton/45% rayon, 1.75 oz (50 g)/55 yds (50 m), small coaster shown in 01 Fuchsia/Red/Green; large coaster shown in 04 Black/Blue/Green
NEEDLES	US 7 (4.5 mm) straight needles or size you need to obtain correct gauge
GAUGE	16 stitches = 4" (10 cm) in pattern
OTHER SUPPLIES	Three stitch markers; 22 charms for small coaster, 28 for large

Getting Started

Thread charms onto yarn.

Cast on 68 stitches, sliding up a charm after every third stitch.

Row 1 (wrong side): Knit all stitches, placing a marker after stitches 17, 34, and 51. The markers are positioned at the middle of three sides of the square and help you keep count.

Note: Slip markers on every row.

Row 2: (K7, sl 1, K2tog, psso, K7) four times.

Rows 3 and all odd-numbered rows through 13: Knit.

Row 4: (K6, sl 1, K2tog, psso, K6) four times.

Row 6: (K5, sl 1, K2tog, psso, K5) four times.

Row 8: (K4, sl 1, K2tog, psso, K4) four times.

Row 10: (K3, sl 1, K2tog, psso, K3) four times.

Row 12: (K2, sl 1, K2tog, psso, K2) four times.

Row 14: (K1, sl 1, K2tog, psso, K1) four times, removing the markers as you go.

Cut the yarn, leaving an 18" tail. Thread tail onto tapestry needle and draw through remaining stitches twice. Pull up snug and fasten off. Sew seam from center to edge.

Finishing

Weave in ends.

Optional Larger Coaster

Thread 28 charms on yarn.

Cast on 84 stitches, sliding up a charm after every third stitch.

Proceed as for smaller coaster but begin (K9, sl 1, K2tog, psso, k9) four times and place markers after stitches 21, 42, and 63.

Eros EXtreme Belt . . . .

Thits "belt" may be tied around your head, neck, waist, or hips—whatever part of you needs embellishment! Simple but elegant is the theme here.

Photo, p. 119

MEASUREMENTS	Approximately 2" (5 cm) wide and 56" (142 cm) long, excluding fringe
YARN	Plymouth, Eros Extreme, 100% nylon, 3.5 oz (100 g)/98 yd (90 m), 777 Multicolor
NEEDLES	US 7 (4.5 mm) straight needles or size you need to obtain correct gauge
GAUGE	Approximately 5 stitches = 4" (10 cm) in pattern
OTHER SUPPLIES	One US G/6 (4.5 mm) crochet hook, 18 beads for fringe

Designed by
Carol Smith

Submitted by
Knit, Purl, & Beyond
Wolfeboro Falls, NH

Variety Is the Spice of Life: Novelty Yarns

Making the Fringe

Cut eight strips of yarn, 12" long.

Knitting the Belt

Cast on 10 stitches, leaving a 6" tail.

Rows 1–4: Knit.

Row 5: *K1, wrap ribbon around needle twice; repeat from *.

Row 6: Knit, dropping the double yarnovers.

Repeat Rows 1–6 to desired length until you're almost out of yarn. Bind off, leaving a 6" tail.

Adding the Fringe

Attach one bead to tail and knot below the bead. *Fold 12" strip of yarn in half, insert crochet hook through end of belt between Rows 2 and 3, catch loop of folded strip and draw through belt; bring two ends through loop and draw up tight. Place bead on each fringe and knot below the bead. Repeat from * three more times evenly across edge. Repeat for other end of belt.

Golden Fantasy

This bag has beads set only every four rows, making it a bit easier to knit than bags with beads set every row. The fringe uses a "crossover" skill: beading with a beading needle and thread.

MEASUREMENTS Approximately 3.25" (8.5 cm) wide and 4" (10 cm) tall, without fringe

YARN Lion Brand Lamé, 65% rayon/35% metalized polyester, 0.67 oz (19 g)/75 yds (67 m), Gold

NEEDLES US 2 (2.75 mm) straight needles or size you need to obtain correct gauge and size 10 steel crochet hook

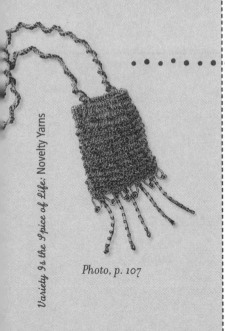

Photo, p. 107

GAUGE	15 stitches = 2" (5 cm) in stockinette stitch
OTHER SUPPLIES	About 400 (two strands from a hank) size 6/0 Czech pony beads in Rainbow Dark Topaz; for fringe, 180 silk finish size 11/0 brass seed beads, 80 silver-lined gold bugle beads; tapestry needle, beading needle, thread
ABBREVIATIONS	KB Knit bead

Designed by
Carol F. Mason Metzger
CFM Designs

Submitted by
My Sister's Knits
Chicago, IL

Getting Started

String the pony beads onto the yarn, reserving 20 beads, 10 each for rows 27 and 51.

Using the backward loop method (see Glossary, page 228), cast on 28 stitches, slide bead, *cast on 4 stitches, slide bead; repeat from * three more times, cast on 3 stitches. You now have 47 stitches and 5 beads.

Row 1: K3, *cast on 1, K4; repeat from * three more times, cast on 1, K28. You now have 52 stitches.

Row 2: Knit.

Row 3: Knit.

Row 4: Knit.

Rows 5, 9, 13, 17, 21, 25, and 29: K1, P50, K1.

Row 6 and all even-numbered rows: Knit.

Rows 7, 11, 15, 19, and 23: Knit, sliding beads between stitches per Golden Fantasy Chart (see page 207).

Row 27: *K3, KB (see Knitting with Beads, page 206), K4; repeat from * eight more times, KB, K3.

Rows 28–30: Knit.

Repeat Rows 7–30 one more time. Bind off 50 stitches, leaving 2 end stitches live for strap.

Knitting the Spiral Strap

Row 1: Place 2 live stitches on needle, K1, slide bead, K1, turn.

Knitting with Beads

The method used for most of this bag leaves a bead or beads lying between two stitches. After completing a stitch, slide a bead up next to the right needle and work the next stitch with the yarn coming out of the bead. The beads will rest on the back of the knitting, which will become the right side when you sew the bag together.

On Row 27, you will put a bead onto a stitch, abbreviated in the pattern as KB, as follows: Put a bead on crochet hook. Remove the next stitch from the left needle with the crochet hook, slide the bead over the stitch, and replace the stitch on the left needle. Now knit this stitch through the back loop.

Row 2: K2.

Repeat Rows 1 and 2 until strap is desired length, or about 28"; I stopped when I ran out of beads. Fasten end to middle of bag at the top.

Finishing

Sew side seam of bag using a whole stitch from each side.

Adding the Fringe

Short Fringe

Step 1: Thread a beading needle, secure thread to inside of bag at lower-right corner, and come through to the outside of the bag.

Step 2: String 9 seed beads, 1 pony bead, and 7 seed beads. Pass through the pony bead again, string 9 seed beads, attach to bag.

Step 3: Pass back through the last bead added, add 3 seed beads, go through pony bead of cast-on row, add 4 seed beads, attach to bag.

Step 4: Pass back through last bead added, string 8 seed beads, 1 pony bead, and 7 seed beads. Pass through the pony bead again, string 9 seed beads, attach to bag.

Repeat Steps 3 and 4 four more times to finish at opposite corner of bag.

Long Fringe

Step 1: Thread a beading needle, secure thread to inside of bag near lower-right corner, come through to outside and pass through last seed bead added in Step 2 and first 3 seed beads and 1 pony bead added in Step 3 of Short Fringe from right to left.

Step 2: Add (1 bugle bead, 1 pony bead) eight times.

Step 3: Add 1 bugle bead, pass back through second-to-last pony bead, (add 1 bugle bead and pass back through next pony bead) six times.

Step 4: Add 1 bugle bead, pass through 1 pony bead and last 4 seed beads added in Step 3 of Short Fringe from right to left.

Step 5: Run needle through inside of bag and come out through the next set of 4 seed beads and 1 pony bead.

Repeat Steps 2–5 three more times and Steps 2–4 one more time to finish the fringe. Secure thread and fasten off.

Golden Fantasy Chart

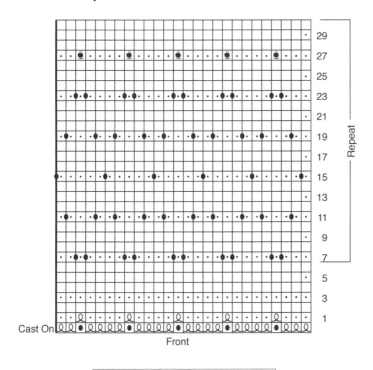

Front

KEY

☐	knit on RS rows; purl on WS rows
·	purl on RS rows; knit on WS rows
ℚ	e-wrap
●	bead between stitches
☻	bead on stitch

Photo, p. 102

Designed by
Camille Meyer

Submitted by
Clickity Sticks & Yarns
Minneapolis, MN

Honey Tangerine Scarf

This simply sophisticated scarf will go anywhere you want to go. Paired with an evening gown, the metallic yarn will add sparkle to any soirée. It also looks divine with a T-shirt and jeans. Dress it up, dress it down, you can't go wrong.

MEASUREMENTS Approximately 10" (25.5 cm) wide and 80" (203 cm) long, unstretched

YARN Feza Night, 80% viscose/20% metallic, 3.5 oz (100 g)/187 yds (170 m)

NEEDLES US 10.5 (6.5 mm) straight needles or size you need to obtain correct gauge

GAUGE 14 stitches = 4" (10 cm) in pattern, unstretched

Knitting the Scarf

Cast on 37 stitches.

Scallop Row: *P2, cast on 1 with backward loop cast-on (see Glossary, page 228), bind off the next 3 stitches; repeat from * to last stitch, P1. You now have 24 stitches.

Next and Following Rows: *P2tog, yo; repeat from * to last stitch, P1.

Continue in pattern to desired length, or until you're almost out of yarn.

Last Row Before Bind-off: P2, *cast on 3 with backward loop cast-on, P1, K2tog, put back onto left needle, K2tog; repeat from *.

Bind off.

Finishing

Weave in ends.

Sheri's Button Bag.........

They won't miss you coming with this baby thrown over your shoulder! Knitted with one of the wildest novelty yarns available, this hot-pink wonder will hold what you need, from car keys to lipstick and many things in between.

Photo, p. 114

Designed by
Sheri Pitroski

Submitted by
The Yarn Patch
Fairfield Glade, TN

MEASUREMENTS	Approximately 9" (23 cm) wide and 7" (18 cm) tall
YARN	Sirdar Fizz, rayon/acrylic/nylon/polyester, 1.75 oz (50 g)/82 yds (75 m), 795 Carnival
NEEDLES	US 8, 9, or 10 (5, 5.5 or 6 mm) straight needles and crochet hook size E/4 (3.5 mm) or F/5 (4.0 mm)
GAUGE	As desired
OTHER SUPPLIES	8 yds plain yarn in similar color for seaming and drawstring; 1 jumbo button with four holes

Knitting the Bag

Cast on 35 stitches.

Knit every row until piece is approximately twice as long as it is wide.

Bind off.

Making the Drawstring (make 2)

With crochet hook and plain yarn, chain 100.

Beginning in second chain from hook, slip stitch in each chain back to the beginning.

Fasten off.

Finishing

Fold bag in half and sew side seams with plain yarn. Attach one end of one drawstring to a safety pin. Beginning at center front top of bag, weave drawstring around top edge in and out of knitting at 1" intervals spaced evenly around, exiting the same hole you started in. Do the same with the second drawstring, but begin at center back.

Slide each of the four drawstring ends through a hole in the button from the back side of the button. Push button down against the bag to make sure drawstrings are not twisted. Knot two ends together twice, or all four together if you like.

Line with fabric if desired.

Jan's Sensational Scarf

The pattern stitch for this lacy scarf is worked on a multiple of 3 plus 2 stitches, so by adding or subtracting 3 or any multiple of 3 stitches, you can knit a narrower or wider scarf. Each row starts and ends with a knit stitch, making a clean edge. This lace looks great in almost any yarn and in any gauge.

Photo, p. 117

Submitted by
Woolcott & Co.
Cambridge, MA

MEASUREMENTS	Approximately 7" (18 cm) wide and 70" (178 cm) long
YARN	Stacy Charles Ritratto, 28% mohair/53% rayon/10% nylon/9% polyester, 1.75 oz (50 g)/198 yds (181 m), Color 77
NEEDLES	US 15 (10 mm) straight needles or size you need to obtain correct gauge
GAUGE	11 stitches = 4" (10 cm) in pattern, unstretched

Knitting the Scarf

Loosely cast on 23 stitches.

Row 1: K1, *K1, yo, K2tog; repeat from * to last stitch, K1.

Repeat this row until scarf is desired length.

Bind off.

Weave in ends.

Catch-all Bowl......................

Photo, p. 103

E veryone needs a catch-all bowl. Coins, paper clips, the buttons that fall off your clothing—they all need a place to call home, at least temporarily. This attractive and colorful bowl can sit on any shelf and will look quite smart while holding your odds and ends. Tightly crocheted in a novelty "cord," the bowl should serve you for many years.

Designed by
Leanne Walker

Submitted by
KnitWit Yarn Shop
Portland, ME

MEASUREMENTS	3.75" (9.5 cm) wide at base and 2.25" (5.5 cm) tall
YARN	Noro Daria Multi, 55% cotton/45% rayon, 1.75 oz (50 g)/55 yd (50 m), Color 17
NEEDLES	One US D/3 (3 mm) crochet hook or size you need to obtain correct gauge
GAUGE	19 stitches = 4" (10 cm) in pattern
ABBREVIATIONS	ch Chain (see Glossary, page 229) sc Single crochet (see Glossary, page 234) sl st Slip stitch (see Glossary, page 234)

Crocheting the Base

Round 1: Ch 4, join with sl st to form a ring, ch 1, sc 7 in ring, join with sl st to beginning ch1.

Round 2: Ch 1, sc 1 in first stitch, sc 2 in each remaining stitch. Join with sl st to beginning ch1. You now have 16 stitches.

Round 3: Ch 1, *1 sc in first stitch, 2 sc in next stitch; repeat from *. Join with sl st to beginning ch1. You now have 24 stitches.

Round 4: Ch 1, *1 sc in next 2 stitches, 2 sc in next stitch, 1 sc in next stitch; repeat from *. Join with sl st. You now have 32 stitches.

Round 5: Ch 1, *1 sc in next 3 stitches, 2 sc in next stitch, 1 sc in next stitch; repeat from *. Join with sl st. You now have 40 stitches.

Round 6: Ch 1, *1 sc in next 4 stitches, 2 sc in next stitch, 1 sc in next stitch; repeat from *. Join with sl st. You now have 48 stitches.

Round 7: Ch 1, *1 sc in next 2 stitches, 2 sc in next stitch, 1 sc in next 4 stitches; repeat from *. Join with sl st. You now have 56 stitches.

Round 8: Ch 1, *1 sc in next 5 stitches, 2 sc in next stitch, 1 sc in next 2 stitches; repeat from *. Join with sl st. You now have 64 stitches.

Crocheting the Sides

Ch 1, sc into the back loop of each of the 64 stitches you have just made. Join with sl st to beginning ch1. *Ch 1, sc in each st around, join with sl st; repeat from * until bowl measures 2".

Work 1 row reverse sc (see Glossary, page 233) around the rim.

Draw yarn tail through final stitch and weave in end.

Photo, p.112

Pandora Scarf

Here's a twist on the novelty yarn scarf—this one is knit on the bias and is a lovely showcase for this fuzzy/shiny/puffy yarn.

MEASUREMENTS	Approximately 3.75" (9.5 cm) wide and 42" (106.5 cm) long
YARN	Trendsetter Pandora, 100% polyamide, 1.75 oz (50 g)/99 yds (90 m), 52 Teal
NEEDLES	US 13 (9 mm) straight needles or size you need to obtain correct gauge
GAUGE	Approximately 16 stitches = 4" (10 cm) in garter stitch

Knitting the Scarf

Cast on 15 stitches.

Row 1: Kfb, knit to last 2 stitches, K2tog.

Designed by
Annelie Wallbom

Submitted by
Hilltop Yarn
Seattle, WA

Row 2: Knit.

Repeat Rows 1 and 2 to desired length, or until you have only enough yarn left to bind off.

Finishing

Weave in ends.

Topless Hat and Fingerless Mittens . . . .

Need just a little warmth without being smothered in yarn? This crocheted open-ended duo will fit the bill. The topless hat has earflaps and ties that can be functional or just left to dangle. The mittens have a thumb slot so they'll stay in place.

Designed by
Jenny Willey

Submitted by
Clickity Sticks & Yarns
Minneapolis, MN

MEASUREMENTS	**Topless Hat:** 22" (56 cm) circumference
	Fingerless Mittens: 7" (18 cm) long and 8" (20.5 cm) around
YARN	South West Trading Company, Pagoda, 100% polyester, 3.5 oz (100 g)/109 yds (100 m), 318 Purple
NEEDLES	One size K/10.5 (7.0 mm) and one size M/13 (9.0 mm) crochet hook or size you need to obtain correct gauge
GAUGE	8.5–9 half double crochet = 4" (10 cm)
ABBREVIATIONS	ch Chain (see Glossary, page 229)
	hdc Half double crochet (see Glossary, page 229)
	sc Single crochet (see Glossary, page 234)
	ss Slip stitch (see Glossary, page 234)

Fingerless Mittens

Crocheting the Mittens

Row 1: With larger hook, ch 15, slip stitch to first chain to form a ring.

Change to smaller hook.

Rounds 2–7: Ch 2,14 hdc, slip stitch into ch2 space.

Round 8: Ch 2, 6 hdc, 2 hdc in next stitch, 1 hdc, 2 hdc in next stitch, 6 hdc, slip stitch into ch2 space.

Round 9: Ch 2, 6 hdc, 2 hdc in next stitch, 3 hdc, 2 hdc in next stitch, 6 hdc, slip stitch into ch2 space.

Round 10: Ch 2, 6 hdc, 2 hdc in next stitch, 5 hdc, 2 hdc in next stitch, 6 hdc, slip stitch into ch2 space.

Round 11: Ch 4, skip 2 hdc, 18 hdc.

Rounds 12–14: 20 sc.

Cut yarn and weave in ends.

Forming the Thumb

Attach yarn at the ch4 space. Ch 1, 8 sc around the space, slip stitch to join. Repeat round once more. Cut yarn and weave in ends.

Topless Hat

Getting Started

Round 1: With larger hook, ch 45, slip stitch to first chain to form a ring.

Change to smaller hook.

Rounds 2–5: Ch 2, 44 hdc, slip stitch into ch2 space.

Crocheting the Earflaps

Right Earflap

Ch 2, 7 hdc, turn, ch 2, 7 hdc, turn, ch 1, dec 1 hdc, 3 hdc, dec 1 hdc (5 stitches remain). Ch 1, turn, dec 1 hdc, 1 hdc, dec 1 hdc (3 stitches remain). Ch 1, turn, work next 3 stitches as 1 hdc (7 loops on hook) (2 stitches decreased, 1 stitch remains), ch1.

Slip stitch 4 along left edge of earflap, 19 hdc along front.

Left Earflap

Repeat instructions for right earflap and slip stitch along left edge of earflap, 12 hdc across back, slip stitch into ch2 space; slip stitch along right side of right earflap.

Do not cut yarn.

Making the Ties

With yarn still attached to right earflap, ch 30. Cut yarn, pull end through last loop, and weave in end. Attach yarn to right side of left earflap, slip stitch to point, ch 30, cut yarn, pull end through last loop, and weave in ends.

Sheri's Crystal FX Evening Bag............

All that glitters is not gold—this glitter is at once a fashionable accessory and a practical handbag. This one has a chain handle, but you could use any fancy cord or braid.

MEASUREMENTS	Approximately 7" (18 cm) wide and 6" (15 cm) tall
YARN	Berroco Crystal FX, 100% nylon, 1.75 oz (50 g)/146 yds (134 m), 4866 Tea and Sympathy
NEEDLES	US 8 (5 mm) straight needles or size you need to obtain correct gauge

Decrease

To decrease in hdc, wrap yarn, draw up loop in next stitch (3 loops on hook); wrap yarn and draw up loop in next stitch to begin second hdc—5 loops on hook. Wrap yarn and draw up loop through all 5 loops on hook—2 hdc become 1.

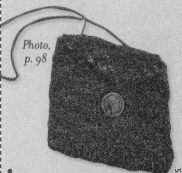

Photo, p. 98

Designed by
Sheri Pitroski

Submitted by
The Yarn Patch
Fairfield Glade, TN

Variety Is the Spice of Life: Novelty Yarns

GAUGE 18 stitches = 4" (10 cm) in pattern

OTHER SUPPLIES Size G/6 (4.5 mm) crochet hook; one 1¼" (3.2 cm) button; 1 yd (1 m) fancy cord, braid, or chain; 12.5" (31.5 cm) × 14.5" (37 cm) piece of lining fabric (optional)

Getting Started

Cast on 36 stitches.

Rows 1, 3, and 5: *K4, P4; repeat from * to last 4 stitches, K4.

Rows 2, 4, and 6: *P4, K4; repeat from * to last 4 stitches, P4.

Rows 7, 9, and 11: Repeat Row 2.

Rows 8, 10, and 12: Repeat Row 1.

Repeat Rows 1–12 until piece measures approximately 12".

Knitting the Flap

Work Rows 1–6, above.

Row 7: Ssk, continue in pattern to last 2 stitches, K2tog.

Continue in pattern, decreasing 1 stitch at the beginning and end of every odd-numbered row until you have 2 stitches.

Knit 2 remaining stitches together. Do not cut yarn.

Making the Button Loop

Place remaining stitch on crochet hook. Chain 15 (more or less, depending on size of button).

Turn, slip stitch in each chain stitch back to beginning.

Join to form a button loop, fasten off.

Finishing

Weave in ends.

Make a fabric lining if desired and tack to inside of bag. Secure strap or chain to top sides of bag. Sew on button.

Victorian Collar·············

This elegant collar is a great way to use that ribbon yarn you've been eyeing. A welcome alternative to the rectangular scarf! The collar is knitted in garter stitch with short-row shaping.

Designed by
Rita Bobry

Submitted by
Downtown Yarns
New York, NY

Photo, p. 105

MEASUREMENTS	Approximately 10" (25 cm) wide and 3" (7.5 cm) deep at the front and 5.5" (14 cm) deep at the back
YARN	Great Adirondack Charmeuse, 100% rayon, 1.75 oz (50 g)/72 yds (66 m)
NEEDLES	US 10.5 (6.5 mm) straight needles or size you need to obtain correct gauge
GAUGE	14 stitches = 4" (10 cm) in pattern
OTHER SUPPLIES	Crochet hook size J/10 (6 mm), one 1" button

Getting Started

Cast on 70 stitches.

Knit 16 rows.

Shaping with Short Rows

First Short Rows: K43 and turn, K16 and turn, K16 and turn.

Next Row: Knit to 1 stitch before the gap, K2tog, turn.

Repeat this row until you have 15 stitches.

Knit 1 row. Bind off.

Finishing

Crochet four shells along front collar edge as follows by making 3 double crochet in each hole (4 total).

Sew on button, using one of the holes formed by the shell stitch as a buttonhole.

Photo, p. 114

Designed by
Tamara Del Sonno

Submitted by
Clickity Sticks & Yarns
Minneapolis, MN

Double Decrease

Slip 2 stitches together knitwise onto right needle. Knit the next stitch. Slip 2 previously slipped stitches together over knitted stitch. The center stitch should lie on top.

Pink Aura Scarf

This pattern is a fine example of how different yarns work up. Both scarves were knitted with the same pattern, yet one is chunky and bold, the other light as a feather. Experiment with different yarns to get just the right look for you.

Variation One

MEASUREMENTS	Approximately 8.5" (21.5 cm) wide and 60" (152.5 cm) long
YARN	Anny Blatt, Muguet, 100% polyamide, 1.75 oz (50 g)/219 yds (200 m), 546 Souris (Smile)
NEEDLES	US 10.5 (6.5 mm) straight needles or size you need to obtain correct gauge
GAUGE	12–16 stitches = 4" (10 cm) over pattern. Knit loosely to encourage drape.

Variation Two

MEASUREMENTS	Approximately 5" (12.5 cm) wide and 58" (147.5 cm) long
YARN	Crystal Palace, Deco-Stardust, 55% lurex/45% nylon, 1.75 oz (50 g)/119 yds (108 m), #4000 Silver
NEEDLES	US 10.5 (6.5 mm) straight needles or size you need to obtain correct gauge
GAUGE	12–16 stitches = 4" (10 cm) over pattern. Knit loosely to encourage drape.

Knitting Variation One

Cast on 33 stitches.

Knit 4 rows.

Row 1: K3, *yo, double decrease, yo, K1; repeat to last 2 stitches, K2.

Row 2: Knit.

Repeat Rows 1 and 2 until you have about 4 yards of yarn left, knit 3 rows, bind off.

Knitting Variation Two

Cast on 21 stitches.

Knit 1 row.

Row 1: K1, *yo, double decrease, yo, K1; repeat from *.

Row 2: Knit.

Repeat Rows 1 and 2 until you have about ½ yard of yarn left, knit 1 row, bind off.

Finishing

Weave in ends.

Infinity Barrette ·············

Here's a novel item for those of you with lots of hair. And you can knit almost a dozen from one skein of hemp, so share them with your friends.

Photo, p. 106

Designed by
Megan Wright

Submitted by
Hilltop Yarn
Seattle, WA

MEASUREMENTS	Approximately 5" (12.5 cm) wide and 2" (5 cm) tall
YARN	Hemp for Knitting All Hemp, 100% hemp, 3.25 oz (90 g)/150 yds (137 m)
NEEDLES	US 2 (2.75 mm) straight needles and two US 2 (2.75 mm) double-point needles (for I-cord) or size you need to obtain correct gauge
GAUGE	20 stitches = 4" (10 cm) in stockinette stitch
OTHER SUPPLIES	Tapestry needle, hair stick, spray starch (optional)

Getting Started

Cast on 24 stitches.

Rows 1–3: Knit.

Row 4 (wrong side): K2, purl to last 2 stitches, K2.

Row 5: Knit.

Row 6: Repeat Row 4.

Row 7: K8, yo, K8, yo, K8. You now have 26 stitches.

Rows 8 and 10: Repeat Row 4.

Rows 9 and 11: Knit.

Rows 12 and 13: Knit.

Bind off on wrong side.

Knitting the I-cord

Using double-point needles, cast on 3 stitches.

Work 3-stitch I-cord (see Glossary, page 229) for 11". Bind off.

Sew the ends of the I-cord, forming a loop.

Finishing

Using photograph on page 219 as a guide, sew I-cord to barrette, being careful not to cover the holes for the hair stick.

Weave in end. Starch if desired.

Contributors

Adirondack Yarns

2241 Saranac Ave., Suite 3
Lake Placid, NY 12946
513.523.9230

Owner and designer: Sue Coffrin

Adirondack Yarns is located in the heart of the Adirondack Mountains in the Olympic Village of Lake Placid, New York. Knitters can find high-quality local and international specialty yarns from the traditional to the unique. There is a large selection of yarns, needles, accessories, crochet supplies, books, and patterns. The friendly staff is always eager to please, and while you shop, knit, or relax, you can enjoy the adjoining full-service coffee shop with a cappuccino and homemade biscotti.

Bella Filati Luxury Yarns

275 B N.E. Broad St.
Southern Pines, NC 28387
910.692.3528
allison@bellafilati.com

Owner: Allison McLean
Designers: Sarah Marie Fuchs and Ryan Anderson (needle felting)

Bella Filati Luxury Yarns has proved to be a destination point for knitters, crocheters, and fiber artists across North Carolina. Nestled in the quaint town of Southern Pines, the store is staffed by a group of women affectionately referred to as "Bella's Babes." These Babes enjoy sharing their passion for fibers and fashion, paired with the tradition of knitting and crochet, with customers of all ages. As soon as customers walk through the doors, their creative wheels turn as they fondle the yarns and admire the models that adorn the shop. At Bella Filati, knitting is not what it used to be.

Cheryl Oberle Designs

3315 Newton St.
Denver, CO 80211
oberleknits@earthlink.net
www.cheryloberle.com

Owner and designer: Cheryl Oberle

At Cheryl Oberle Designs you will find kits, designs, and yarn created for your knitting pleasure. Both Dancing Colors and Reflections Yarn are a blend of merino and mohair that is wonderfully soft and lustrous. Each skein is hand-dyed individually by Ms. Oberle herself. In this way she ensures accurate color replication without compromising the unique "personality" of each skein. Because each skein is unique, so is each Dancing Colors or Reflections garment.

Clickity Sticks & Yarns

2722 East 50th St.
Minneapolis, MN 55417
612.724.2500

Owner and designer: Tamara Del Sonno
Designers: Kirsten Avent, Anne Bieter Lenzini, Camille Meyer, Bernadette St. Amant, Pat Taylor, and Jenny Willey

Craftique/Never Enough Knitting

119-121 N. Main St.
Wheaton, IL 60187
630.221.1007

Owners and designers: Jean Austin and Jane M. Brown

Craftique/Never Enough Knitting is located in Chicago's western suburbs. Craftique specializes in quilting supplies and reproduction fabrics. Never Enough Knitting is a full-service yarn shop where special orders are always welcome and assistance with projects is free. Special sale dates occur three times each year, offering a 20 percent discount on all yarn, notions, and fabric purchases, including special orders.

Dorothy T. Ratigan

Dorothy T. Ratigan's career in fiber arts spans 30 years, as a shop owner, designer, and technical editor. One of her designs is featured in *The Vogue Knitting Book*.

Downtown Yarns

45 Avenue A
New York, NY 10009
212.995.5991
downtownyarns45@verizon.net

Owner and designer: Rita Bobry

Downtown Yarns is a neighborhood store dedicated to encouraging handcrafting activities such as knitting and crocheting. The store offers a large range of natural fibers and novelty yarns, as well as classes taught on all levels.

The Dragonfly Yarn Shop

1327 N. Wright Rd., Suite 5A
Janesville, WI 53546
608.757.9228

Owner and designer: Kerri A. Shank

The Dragonfly Yarn Shop offers Cascade, Knit One, Crochet Two, Ironstone, Misti Alpaca, Blue Heron, Debbie Bliss, Knitting Fever, and Louisa Harding yarns. Open since September 2004, this small shop offers lessons by the hour.

Enticements

135 E. Prairie Ave.
Decatur, IL 62523
217.422.5870
floburd@insightbb.com

Owners and designers: Flo Burdick and Kristine Hardy

Enticements has knitting, cross-stitch, and needlework accessories. Many classes are offered year-round and an in-house designer is always available for assistance. Also available is a large selection of sterling jewelry. Enticements will be relocating in September 2006 to downtown Decatur, at 135 East Prairie Avenue, Decatur, IL 62523.

Fiberworks

4013 Dayton-Xenia Rd.
Dayton (Beavercreek), OH 45432-1902
937.231.2768
Fibrwrks@aol.com
www.fiberworksdayton.blogspot.com

Owner and designer: Arlene Graham

Fiberworks has something for fiberholics of every stripe: hand-spun and hand-painted yarns, spinning and felting fibers, equipment, select luxury yarns, a comprehensive selection of fiber arts books, and a wide assortment of needles, notions, and novelties. Additionally, a variety of classes and groups are offered, including knitting, spinning, and felting; all meet in a cozy and supportive environment where advice and chocolate are always at hand.

Grafton Yarn Store

1300 14th Ave.
Grafton, WI 53024
262.377.0344
www.graftonyarnstore.com

Owner and designer: Ann Schantz

The Grafton Yarn Store is located in the historic Grafton Mill along the scenic Milwaukee River. Once home to the Badger Woolen Mills, the shop has operated as a retail source for specialty yarns since 1961. In addition to a large classroom, the Grafton Yarn Store offers a comfy seating area where all are welcome to drop by and knit with owner Anna Schantz. Quarterly newsletters feature original patterns, upcoming classes, and contests. Perhaps the Grafton Yarn Store's best asset is instructor Mildred Schumacher, who worked at the Badger Mills over 50 years ago. This is a yarn store that embraces both new and old-school traditions.

Green Mountain Spinnery

Box 568
Putney, VT 05346
802.387.4528
spinnery@sover.net
www.spinnery.com

Designers: Margaret Atkinson, Diana Lischer Goodband, and Claire P. Wilson

The Spinnery was established in 1981 to spin local fleece into the finest possible yarn for knitters and weavers. Since those early days the shop has expanded its scope, introducing GREENSPUN processing and spinning blends of wool and precious fiber — silk, llama, mohair — while still producing sturdy 100% New England wool yarns in a rainbow of dyed and natural colors.

The Spinnery's founding principles are to conduct business in a democratic and environmentally responsible manner. All long-term workers at the Spinnery participate in setting purposes and policies, and approximately a quarter of the workforce owns the business.

Harvest Moon Handspun

24 7th St.
York, SC 29745
803.628.6809

Designer: Sue Dial

Sue Dial got her first spinning wheel in 1988 and has been knitting exclusively with her own handspun yarn ever since. She raises angora rabbits and, whenever possible, she uses their fiber, along with fiber from her dogs and other locally produced animal fibers in her work. She's happy to receive custom spinning, knitting, and/or dyeing orders. Her designs were submitted by Baskets of Yarn, Charlotte, NC (704-561-0911), a retail knit, crochet, and fiber arts supply and teaching company. The store carries yarns from around the world, as well as handspun and hand-dyed yarns from local fiber artists. They offer a variety of classes, camps, retreats, workshops, and cruises throughout the year.

Haus of Yarn

Paddock Place
73 White Bridge Rd.
Nashville, TN 37205
615.354.1007

Owner and designer: Carolyn J. Smith
Designers: Bobbe Morris and Leah Oakley

Opened in 2003, Haus of Yarn is a full-service knit and crochet center with the most varied and comprehensive yarn selection in Middle Tennessee. Knit by staff members and displayed throughout the store, models help one select yarns and patterns, as well as spark creativity. The friendly staff have more than 250 combined years of knitting experience, so you can trust them to accurately answer any knitting questions. Classes are offered for knitters of all skills and ages. Customers enjoy the cozy atmosphere, the helpful and courteous staff, competitive prices, and an incomparable selection of patterns, books, needles, accessories, and, of course, yarn.

Hilltop Yarn

2224 Queen Anne Ave. North
Seattle, WA 98109
206.282.1332

Owner and designer: Jennifer Hill
Designers: Kathryn Connelly, Alexandra Immel, Tatyana Tchibova, Annelie Wallbom, and Megan Wright

Housed in a craftsman mansion on Seattle's Queen Anne Hill, Hilltop Yarn is a jewel box of colorful yarns nestled in original kitchen cabinets and library bookshelves. During warmer months, you'll find knitters, needles flying, seated in Adirondack chairs on covered porches. During colder months, Hilltop fans head indoors to secret spots like the cozy library replete with afghans and doilies created by the owner's grandmothers, Ester and Norene. The shop offers special events, including fashion shows, book signings, exclusive Knit Kits, and classes.

Judith Durant

Judith Durant is a founding editor of *Interweave Knits* magazine, author of *Never Knit Your Man a Sweater* (Storey Publishing), and co-author of *The Beader's Companion*.

Kaolin Designs

727 Archie Whitesides Rd.
Gastonia, NC 28052
704.854.9072
kaolindesigns@earthlink.net

Owner and designer: Linda O'Leary

Kaolin Designs offers a selection of hand-painted yarns for the hand-knitter and crocheter. The shop also offers wools, mohairs, and silk blends, as well as hand-painted wool rovings and kits; custom color orders are welcome.

Knit-Knot Studio

1238 NW Glisan St., Suite A
Portland, OR 97209
503.222.3818
knitknotstudio@yahoo.com

Owner and designer: Elizabeth Prusiewicz

Knit-Knot Studio is a small store in the heart of the historic Pearl District of Portland, Oregon, where you can find colorful yarns as well as books, classes, and help on your projects. Owner Elizabeth Prusiewicz designs beautiful hats, sweaters, scarves, and other one-of-a-kind items for the store and on request.

Knit, Purl, & Beyond

P.O. Box 1078
36 Center St.
Wolfeboro Falls, NH 03896
603.569.1118

Owner and designer: Carol Smith

Located in the lakes region of New Hampshire, Wolfeboro is a busy resort community on the shores of Lake Winnipesaukee. Knit, Purl, & Beyond is a quality yarn shop in a casual setting with an extensive inventory of both yarns and accessories.

Knitting, Etc.

2255 N. Triphammer Rd.
Triphammer Mall
Ithaca, NY 14850

Owner: Hickory Lee
Designer: Catherine Devine

KnitWit Yarn Shop

247A Congress St.
Portland, ME 04101
207.774.6444

Owners: Anna Poe and Joshua Eckels
Designers: Hannah Fettig, Dierdra Logan, Nancy Miller, Leanne Walker, and Judy Warde

KnitWit Yarn Shop is located in Portland's East End, in a storefront with a high, pressed-tin ceiling, original wood floors, and furniture designed by the owners, Joshua Eckels and Anna Poe. KnitWit offers freshly baked, store-made treats and cappuccino to customers who browse the pattern library or take one of the many classes offered for all levels of knitters. Owned by two artists who love to knit and find interesting fibers to share with customers (including yarns made in Maine), KnitWit is a great place to get a color-and-texture fix, plan your next project, or succumb to temptation and just add to your stash.

Knot Another Hat

202 Yasui Building
16 Oak St.
Hood River, OR 97031
541.308.0002
sarah@knotanotherhat.com

Owner and designer: Sarah B. Keller

Located in the Columbia River Gorge National Scenic Area, Knot Another Hat is a full-service yarn store where you can find anything hip and knitworthy. The shop specializes in fine yarns and needles, as well as the latest patterns, accessories, gifts, and more. You can also find ecological wool, soy yarns, bamboo fibers, locally grown alpaca, and yarn spun in Columbia River Gorge. This shop has an extensive class schedule, ranging from learn-to-knit classes to advanced sweater classes and everything in between. Grab a coffee and bring your latest project to sit and knit in the comfy seating area.

Loop Yarn Shop

2900 S. Delaware Ave.
Milwaukee, WI 53207
414.481.4843

Owners and designers: Patricia Colloton-Walsh and Caitlin Walsh

Loop Yarn Shop dedicates itself to creativity in the use of fibers. A mother/daughter-run business, artist and teacher, with crocheting and knitting loved by both, Loop emphasizes design and learning in its approach to fiber arts. Loop welcomes a diverse Milwaukee population to its colorful, yarn-filled store, which is two blocks from Lake Michigan in the cozy neighborhood of Bayview.

Lowellmountain Wools

194 Mitchell Rd.
Lowell, VT

Owner and designer: Diana Foster

Mad About Ewes

429 Market St.
Lewisburg, PA 17837
570.524.5775

www.madaboutewes.com

Owner: Libby Beiler
Designer: Melanie Wagner

Mad About Ewes Fiber Arts Studio carries yarns and supplies for the knitter and crocheter, as well as fibers and accessories for hand-spinners. Classes are offered in a wide variety of areas, including knitting, crocheting, felting, and hand spinning.

Maggie's Rags

mkr@maggiesrags.com
www.maggiesrags.com

Designer: Margaret K. K. Radcliffe

Maggie's Rags was founded in the spring of 1997. Margaret has been designing handknits since the early 1980s and has taught knitting since 1991, for national organizations such as The Knitting Guild of America and Stitches, on cruise ships, locally at yarn shops and for the YMCA, and for fiber guilds throughout the United States.

Margie's Muse Handweaving & Gallery

3779 Vermont Rte. 30
Jamaica, VT 05343
802.874.7201
margaret@margiesmuse.com

Owner and designer: Margaret Silvia

Margie's Muse Handweaving and Gallery offers custom pieces for body and home created from a variety of luscious local and imported yarns. Come be inspired by knitting classes, knitting and spinning tools, and a colorful, eclectic array of handmade items from over 100 artisans.

Marji's Yarncrafts

381 Salmon Brook St.
Granby, CT 06035
860.653.9700
www.marjisyarncrafts.com

Owner and designer: Marji B. LaFreniere

For 18 years, Marji's Yarncrafts has been carrying a large selection of basics and more, in natural fibers and blends, as well as buttons, needles, and accessories, and classes throughout the year.

My Sister's Knits

9907 S. Walden Parkway
Chicago, IL 60643
773.238.4555

Owner: Carol Oprondek
Designer: Carol F. Mason Metzger (CFM Designs)

An RN of 33 years, Carol Oprondek opened My Sister's Knits in 2005. Named after the owner's sister, Davia, and herself, the shop is in a quaint little neighborhood on the Southwest side of Chicago. Her two golden retrievers, Cody and Goldie, join her at work every day.

Nancy Lindberg

Nancy Lindberg developed her teaching skills while owning a yarn shop in Minneapolis for more than a decade. She moved on to pattern designing and continues to teach, which has garnered a large and faithful following. Her patterns appeal to all knitting levels and are available in yarn shops across the United States.

Rainbow Yarn and Fibres

1980 Exeter Rd.
Germantown, TN 38138
901.753.9835

Owner and designer: Brigitte Lang

Located in an upscale suburb of Memphis, Rainbow Yarn and Fibres offers knitting, crochet, and spinning classes for all levels. Warm, vibrant colors fill the store. Owner Brigitte Lang offers friendly expertise, while designing original patterns and hosting a constant circle of knitters.

Sew Krazy

142 E. Liberty St.
Wooster, OH 44691
330.262.7397
www.sew-krazy.com

Owner: Rina Stein
Designer: Margaret Anne Halas

With a few skeins of gorgeous yarn and a tiny collection of wonderful fabrics, Sew Krazy opened for business in January 2003 in a cozy space tucked away on the upper level of Liberty Street Commons. As the little shop grew and became popular with knitters and quilters from all over Ohio, Michigan, and surrounding states, Sew Krazy relocated to a larger establishment just next door. Come with a project to sit and relax in front of the fireplace, and check out the new fibers and fabrics. The shop also offers knitting, sewing, and quilting classes.

South Pine Ranch

P.O. Box 428
Conifer, CO 80433
303.838.5665
minervalingusky@yahoo.com

Owners: Kathy and Doug Lingusky
Designer: Kathy Lingusky

South Pine Ranch is a small fiber ranch specializing in handspun, hand-knitted clothing and home items. Knitting and spinning lessons are available upon request.

Stash – Yarn + Inspiration

1820 Solano Ave., Suite B-2
Berkeley, CA 94707
510.558.YARN
www.stashyarn.com
knitchic@gmail.com (Jessie)

Owners: Ellen Roosevelt and Nicole Green
Designer: Jessie Dotson

Stash Yarn + Inspiration provides a comfortable, organized environment that invites knitters to browse the displays of yarn, books, and notions or simply to slow down, find a comfortable place to sit and knit, and be inspired by the beautiful yarn surrounding them. Stash is a place with a modern sensibility of an ageless craft.

Stitchy Women

66 Depot St.
Poultney, VT 05764
802.287.4114
stitchywomen@adelphia.net

Owner: Sue Publicover
Designer: Marlee Mason

Contributors

String

1015 Madison Ave.
New York, NY 10021
212.288.9572
www.stringyarns.com

Owner and designer: Linda Morse

Hailed by Zagat's *New York City Shopping Guide* as "the Bergdorf Goodman of knitting stores," String offers an unparalleled collection of high-quality yarns, all saturated with dazzling color and texture. More than a source for distinctive materials, String showcases sophisticated designs inspired by current trends and String's discerning customers' desires. The collection includes wraps, capes, scarves, hats, and, sweaters; baby and children's clothes and accessories; and pillows, throws, and bags. For knitters who can't make into the Madison Avenue location, most products are available online.

Weaving Southwest

216-B Paseo del Pueblo Norte
Taos, NM 87571
505.758.0433
weaving@weavingsouthwest.com

Owner and designer: Pat Dozier

Weaving Southwest offers hand-dyed yarns in six different knitting weights and textures with 34 colors in each. Hand-dyed weaving yarns are also available, along with weaving equipment and spinning wheels; Weaving Southwest manufactures its own looms.

Webs

P.O. Box 147
75 Service Center Rd.
Northampton, MA 01064
800.367.9327
www.yarn.com

Designers: Linda Burt, Sandra Clockedile, Jazmin Greenlaw, Kirsten Hipsky, Karen J. Minott, and Cirilia Rose

Webs, known as America's Yarn Store, is located in the picturesque Pioneer Valley of western Massachusetts. A second-generation family-owned business, Webs has been the destination for knitters, weavers, and spinners for more than 30 years. The store features a 5,000-square-foot retail store and 15,000 square feet of warehouse space that is always open to the public. The warehouse is full of closeouts, mill ends, and odds at incredible prices. The store offers many of the top knitting brands as well as many smaller, unique brands, including its own Valley Yarns line. Besides having a great selection of yarn, Webs is committed to saving you money. Many yarn purchases qualify for a 20- to 25- percent discount. Visit online for a great selection, as well as wonderful discounts.

Whitmore Lake Yarn Company

9535 Main St.
Whitmore Lake, MI 48189
734.449.9688
www.whitmorelakeyarn.com

Owner: Dee Koehler
Designer: Patt Corr

Combine a love for yarn and a passion for the art of knitting and crocheting, place it in an 1873 historic building located in a quaint downtown area, and add the most important ingredient of all — friendship — and you have Whitmore Lake Yarn Company. Here one can find a multitude of yarns, needles, and accessories, as well as books and patterns.

Wool Away

203 Webster St., #3
St. Johnsbury, VT 05819
802.748.5767
miriamtheyarnlady@hotmail.com

Owner and designer: Miriam G. Briggs

Woolcott & Co.

61 JFK St.
Cambridge, MA 02138
617.547.2837
info@woolcottandco.com

Yarn LLC

910 Whalley Ave.
New Haven, CT 06515
www.yarnllc.com

Owners and designers: Toni Kayser Weiner and Linda Colman

Yarn LLC has two locations in the city of New Haven: the original shop in the Westville section and a newer one in the downtown area's designated arts district. Both shops are light-filled and awash with color. They are co-owned by Linda Colman and Toni Kayser Weiner, who bring their vast knowledge and experience in design and textile arts.

Their commitment to providing customers with quality yarn and expert instruction is apparent the moment you step in the front door. The carefully chosen, beautifully displayed inventory includes hand-dyed, hand-painted yarns, classic-name staples, cutting-edge, innovative accent yarns, books, needles, and knitting accessories. The warm and supportive staff is determined to make your knitting projects successful. A visit to this creative space will launch you on an inspired knit journey.

The Yarn Patch

P.O. Box 1737
126 Stonehenge Dr.
Village Green Mall
Fairfield Glade, TN 38558
931.707.1255
knitandfish@earthlink.com

Owner and designer: Sheri Pitroski

The Yarn Patch is a fun and friendly shop with something for every style and season. The shop offers a large variety of quality yarns, tools, and patterns, and is blessed with an experienced and patient staff. Along with fun events when the mood strikes, classes and workshops are offered at every level.

Glossary

Backward loop cast-on. Hold the end of the yarn and a needle in your right hand. Hold the working yarn in your left hand. Bring your left thumb over the top, down behind, and up in front of the yarn to create a loop. Insert needle into loop on thumb as if to knit and slide loop onto needle. You may also use the loop cast-on to add stitches to the end of a row of knitting.

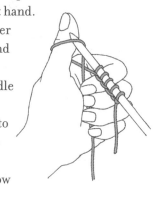

Cable cast-on. Make a slipknot and place it on your left needle. Follow Steps 1 and 2 for knitted cast-on, page 231, then follow Steps 1 and 2 below.

1. Place the second needle between the two stitches on the first needle.

2. Knit a new stitch between the two stitches, pull it long, and place it on the first needle.

Continue in this manner, knitting between the last two stitches on the first needle, until you have the required number of stitches.

Chain (crochet). Begin with a slipknot on the hook. Wrap yarn over hook and pull the loop through the slipknot. Yarn over hook, pull loop through loop on hook to make second chain. Repeat for the required number of chain stitches.

Double crochet. Yarn over hook. Insert hook through both loops of next stitch. Draw loop through stitch. Yarn over hook. Draw loop through first two loops on hook. Yarn over hook. Draw loop through two loops on hook.

Garter stitch. When knitting back and forth in rows, knit all rows. When knitting circularly, knit one row, purl one row.

Half double crochet. Yarn over hook. Insert hook through both loops of next stitch. Yarn over and draw loop through stitch. Yarn over hook and draw through all three loops on hook.

I-cord. Use two double-point needles to make I-cord. Cast on three or four stitches. *Knit all stitches. Without turning work, slide the stitches to the other end of the needle. Pull the working yarn across the back. Repeat from * until cord is desired length. Bind off.

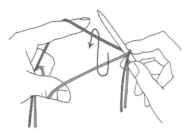

Invisible cast-on. Tie a piece of waste yarn onto the end of your working yarn. With the knot held on top of the needle with your right index finger, hold the yarns in your left hand with the working yarn over your index finger and the waste yarn over your thumb.

1. Bring the needle in front of and under the waste yarn and pick up a loop of the working yarn.

2. Bring the loop under the waste yarn.

3. Now bring the needle over then under the working yarn and pick up a loop.

Repeat Steps 1 through 3 until you have the required number of stitches.

Kitchener stitch. This grafting technique is used to join two sets of live stitches invisibly. It is most often used for sock toes, but can be used to join shoulder seams or two halves of a scarf.

1. Place the two sets of live stitches to be bound off on separate needles. Hold the needles parallel in your left hand with right sides of the knitted fabric touching.

2. Insert the tapestry needle into the first stitch on the front needle as if to knit, and slip the stitch off the needle. Then insert the 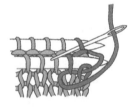 tapestry needle into the next stitch on the front needle as if to purl, and leave the stitch on the needle.

3. Insert the tapestry needle into the first stitch on the back needle as if to purl, and slip the stitch off the needle.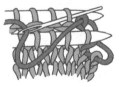

4. Insert the tapestry needle into the next stitch on the back needle as if to knit, and leave the stitch on the needle.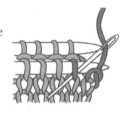

Repeat Steps 2, 3, and 4 until all stitches have been joined.

K2tog bind-off. Knit one stitch and slip the next stitch knitwise. Insert the left needle into the two stitches on the right needle from left to right.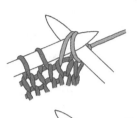

Knit the two stitches together.

Continue until all stitches are bound off. Cut the yarn and pull through last stitch.

Knit the knits and purl the purls. This simply means that you work the stitches as they appear on your needles. For example, if a stitch was knitted on the right-side row, it appears as a purl on the wrong side and should be purled on the wrong-side row.

Knitted cast-on. Make a slipknot and place it on your left needle.

1. Knit a stitch into the slipknot, leaving the slip-knot on the needle.

2. Place the new stitch onto left needle by inserting the left needle into the front of the new stitch.

3. Tighten stitch and continue until you have the required number of stitches.

Knitwise. When a pattern says "slip the next stitch knitwise," insert your needle into the next stitch from front to back as if you were going to knit it, then slip it to the right needle without knitting it.

M1 increase.

1. Work in pattern to where you'll need to begin increasing. Insert the tip of the right needle from back to front underneath the strand of yarn between the two needles and place the lifted strand on the left needle.

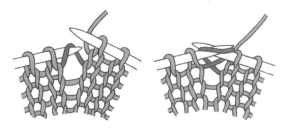

2. Knit the lifted strand through its back loop, twisting it to avoid leaving a hole.

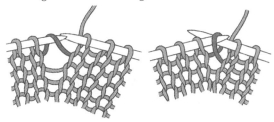

Pompom. Cut a square of cardboard a little larger than the size of the pompom you want to make. Make a slit down the center, stopping just past the center point.

1. Center a 12" piece of yarn in the slit, leaving both ends hanging.

2. Wrap yarn around the cardboard to desired thickness of pompom. Cut the yarn.

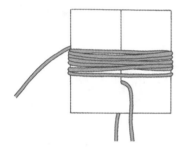

3. Tie the wrapped yarn tightly together with the piece of yarn that's hanging in the slit.

4. Cut the wrapped yarn along both edges of the cardboard.

5. Remove the cardboard, fluff up the pompom, and trim any uneven ends.

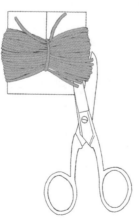

Provisional cast-on (crochet over needle)

1. Make a slip knot and place it on a crochet hook. Hold your knitting needle on top of a long strand of yarn.

2. * With the crochet hook, draw the yarn over the needle and through the loop on the hook. To cast on another stitch, bring yarn behind knitting needle into position as for Step 1, and repeat from *. *Note:* If you find it awkward to cast on the first couple of stitches, work a few crochet chain stitches before casting onto the needle so you have something to hold on to.

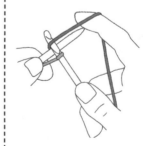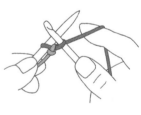

3. When the last stitch has been cast on, work two or three extra crochet chain stitches without taking the yarn around the knitting needle, then cut the yarn, leaving a 10" tail, draw the tail through the last loop on the hook, and pull the tail to close the loop loosely — just enough so the tail can't escape. To remove the scrap yarn when you've finished the knitting, pull the tail out of the last loop and gently tug on it to "unzip" the chain and carefully place the live stitches on a needle, holder, or separate length of scrap yarn as they are released.

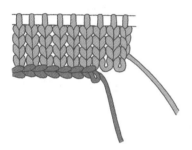

Purlwise. When a pattern says "slip the next stitch purlwise," keep the working yarn to the back and insert your needle into the next stitch from back to front as if you were going to purl it, then slip it to the right needle without purling it.

Reverse single crochet. This is worked the same as single crochet, only you work from left to right. Reverse single crochet creates a "braided" edge.

Seed stitch. This is an alternating K1, P1 stitch. When knitting back and forth, on wrong-side rows knit the stitches that were knit on the right side (they will look like purls on the wrong side) and purl the stitches that were purled on the right side (they will look like knits on the wrong side). When working circularly, purl the stitches that were knit on the previous round and knit the stitches that were purled on the previous round.

Short rows (WT). Work the number of stitches specified; this will leave some stitches unworked at the end of the row. Bring the yarn to the front of the work and slip the next stitch from the left needle to the right needle as if to purl. Bring the yarn to the back again and return the slipped stitch to the left needle. The first stitch on the left needle now has the working yarn wrapped around its base.

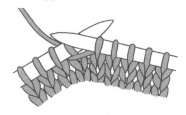

If you're working short rows in stockinette stitch, you'll have to close the gaps and hide the wraps. To hide the wraps on a right-side row, insert the right needle tip under the wrap from front to back and from bottom to top and then into the wrapped stitch as if to knit. Knit the stitch together with its wrap.

To hide the wraps on a wrong-side row, use the right needle tip to lift the back loop of the wrap from back to front and from bottom to top, then place it on the left needle. Purl the stitch together with its wrap.

Single crochet. Insert hook into next stitch, wrap yarn over hook, and draw the loop through the stitch. You now have two loops on the hook. Yarn over hook and draw loop through both loops on hook.

Single crochet decrease. Insert hook into next stitch, wrap yarn over hook and draw the loop through the stitch. Insert hook into next stitch, wrap yarn over hook and draw the loop through the stitch. Yarn over needle and draw through all three loops on hook.

Slip stitch crochet. Insert hook into next stitch, wrap yarn over hook, and draw the loop through the stitch and the loop on the hook.

Stockinette stitch. When knitting back and forth in rows, knit the right-side rows, purl the wrong-side rows. When knitting circularly, knit all rounds.

Suspended bind-off. Knit 2 stitches. *Lift the first stitch over the second stitch as for a regular bind-off but leave the lifted stitch on the left needle. Pass your right needle in front of the suspended stitch, knit the next stitch, and drop both from the left needle. Repeat from * until all stitches are bound off.

Tassel. Cut a rectangle of cardboard a little longer than you want the tassel to be. Wrap the yarn around the cardboard lengthwise to desired thickness of tassel. Cut a 24" piece of yarn and fold it in half. Slide this yarn under the wrapped yarn and up to the top of the cardboard. Tie the two ends tightly around the wrapped yarn.

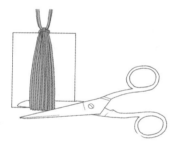

Cut through the wrapped yarn at the bottom end of the tassel.

Cut a 12" piece of yarn and wrap it two or three times tightly around the tassel, about 1" down from the top.

Tie this yarn securely and move the ends to the inside of the tassel. Trim evenly.

Three-needle bind-off. This technique is used to join two sets of live stitches.

1. Place the two sets of stitches to be bound off on separate needles. Hold the needles parallel in your left hand with right sides of the knitted fabric touching.

2. Insert the tip of a third needle into the first stitch on both needles and knit these two stitches together.

3. Repeat Step 2. You now have two stitches on the right needle. With one of the needles in your left hand, lift the first stitch on the right needle over the second and off the needle as for a regular bind-off. Repeat until all stitches are bound off.

Triple Crochet. Yarn over hook twice. Insert hook through both loops of next stitch. Draw loop through stitch. Yarn over hook. Draw loop through first two loops on hook. Yarn over hook. Draw loop through two loops on hook. Yarn over hook. Draw loop through remaining two loops on hook.

Wraps per inch. This is the number of wraps it takes to cover one inch of a ruler with the yarn. The heavier the yarn, the fewer number of times it will wrap around one inch; the finer the yarn, the more times it will wrap.

Glossary

Index

Page numbers in *italics* indicate photographs and drawings.

Other Storey Titles You Will Enjoy

Felt It!, by Maggie Pace.

Hats, shawls, belts, bags, home accessories — the perfect introduction to the magic of felting, for all levels of knitters.
152 pages. Paper. ISBN 1-58017-635-6.

Knit One, Felt Too, by Kathleen Taylor.

Twenty-five spectacular projects to transform items, knit large and loose, into thick, cozy, felted garments or accessories.
176 pages. Paper. ISBN 1-58017-497-3.

Knit Scarves!, by Candi Jensen.

Fifteen patterns for colorful, cozy scarves, plus advice on needle choices and yarn alternatives.
96 pages. Die-cut paper-over-board. ISBN 1-58017-577-5.

Knits Socks!, by Betsy Lee McCarthy.

The latest addition to a best-selling series — fifteen patterns for all levels of knitters, paired with advice on knitting in the round on five needles.
144 pages. Die-cut paper-over-board. ISBN 1-58017-537-6.

The Knitting Answer Book, by Margaret Radcliffe.

Answers for every yarn crisis — an indispensable addition to every knitter's project bag.
400 pages. Flexibind with cloth spine. ISBN 1-58017-599-6.

Knitting Loves Crochet, by Candi Jensen.

A collection of designs where soft, shapely knitting meets pretty, crocheted edgings and flowers.
192 pages. Paper. ISBN 1-58017-842-1.

Knitting Rules!, by Stephanie Pearl-McPhee.

A sourcebook of invaluable advice, woven with witty insights and wry reflections in celebration of the knitting life.
224 pages. Paper. ISBN 1-58017-834-0.

These and other books from Storey Publishing are available
wherever quality books are sold or by calling 1-800-441-5700.
Visit us at *www.storey.com*.